D0065667

NAMELESS

Organizational Change

NAMELESS
Organizational Change

No-Hype, Low-Resistance Corporate Transformation

Glenn Allen-Meyer

with

Neil H. Katz, Ph.D.

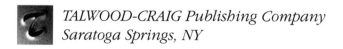

TALWOOD-CRAIG Publishing Company
Saratoga Springs, NY

Substantial discounts on bulk quantities of this book are available to corporations, educational institutions, professional associations, and other organizations. For details and discount information, contact the publisher, Talwood-Craig Publishing Company, P.O. Box 137, Saratoga Springs, NY 12866. Telephone: 518-584-8477. Fax: 810-963-5891. Email: tcpub@mindspring.com.

Publisher's Cataloging-in-Publication *(Provided by Quality Books, Inc.)*

Allen-Meyer, Glenn.
    Nameless organizational change : no-hype, low-resistance corporate transformation / Glenn Allen-Meyer ; with Neil H. Katz. --1st ed.
        p. cm.
        Includes bibliographical references and index.
        LCCN: 99-91251
        ISBN: 0-9675079-0-1

        1. Organizational change.   I. Title.

HD58.5.A55 1999   658.4'06
                                   QBI99-1553

Acknowledgments

An exhaustive rendition of all who have guided, aided, and contributed to the ideas presented in this book would not be possible in the allotted space—such is the derivative nature of all my mind has become. A few special acknowledgments are in order, however.

To my friend and collaborator, Dr. Neil Katz, special words must be spoken. His trust in me over the years has enabled my growth as both a person and as a professional. Thank you, Neil!

The American University/NTL Institute O.D. program tilled fertile ground for the development of ideas, respect for all who have come before me, and a profound appreciation for the impact of the changer in the change. Dr. Robert Marshak provided invaluable advice on the presentation of the ideas contained herein. Dr. Earl Potter, III, Dean of the School of Management at Lesley College in Boston, MA, gave to me the same pointed and accurate feedback about the book he has given so often in my other pursuits.

Col. Edward F. Danowitz, USMC (Ret.), Director of the Combined Action Program (1968-1969), helped with more than just facts regarding a unique approach to change—he gave me a personal sense of justified pride from a difficult time.

In addition to writing this book's Foreword, Frederick A. Miller, President and CEO of The Kaleel Jamison Consulting Group, Inc., helped me understand the degree to which the objectification of change is really the objectification of people (or, perhaps, it's the other way around). This book improved as a result of his coaching.

Nancy Meyer, Jeannette Astor, Margaret LeBrun, and Vanessa Budetti were invaluable as readers and editors. Margo Quinto, an unabashed believer in my writing, offers encouragement that is priceless.

None of the work in this book would have been attempted without the simple support of Chris Jones of the United States Social Security Administration. While her kind words may, for her, have been "all in a day's work," to me they were transformational. Thank you Chris!

The final, and most important of all acknowledgments, are due to Susan Allen-Meyer. Should this past year become our *annus mirabilis*, to you belongs the credit. Your modeling of attachment parenting, an inspiration for much of this book, made it possible for me to be both an author/consultant and a Dad to our most significant named changes, Jasmine and Cianan! Susan, the ideas we share about life, work, and the world inform everything I do.

For Susan
and her patience
with everyone in the world named
"Allen-Meyer"

Table of Contents

FOREWORD
Frederick A. Miller, President and CEO,
The Kaleel Jamison Consulting Group, Inc. ....i-ix

INTRODUCTION 1-12
▼ The Hype of the Traditional Approach to Change 1
  - **Figure 1**: The Traditional Approach to Change 3
▼ Understanding Nameless Change 5
  - **Figure 2**: The Nameless Approach 7

CHAPTER ONE
Current Assumptions About Organizational
Change 13-26
▼ The Assumptions 16
▼ Understanding the Results.....................................21
▼ The Snowball Model 23

CHAPTER TWO
Everyday Stress in Organizations 27-48
▼ The Organizational Monoculture 29
▼ A Brief History of Work 36
▼ The Baseline Level of Stress.....................................46

CHAPTER THREE
Programmatic Methods of Change 49-64
▼ The Commodification of Change...51
▼ Marketing the Changes We Manufacture 58

CHAPTER FOUR
Resistance to Programmatic Change 65-88
▼ Sources of Resistance to Change 66
▼ The Power of Naming 67
▼ Forming an Attachment to Work 70
▼ Cognitive Resistance to Change 74
▼ Liberty as a Barrier to Change 85

CHAPTER FIVE
The Bottom-Line Costs of Resistance 89-122
- ▼ What Change is Like on the Line 90
- ▼ The Pace of Change 93
- ▼ The Stress Study 97
- ▼ The Costs of Organizational Change 101
- ▼ Locking on to Programmatic Change 116

CHAPTER SIX
Finding a Better Way to Change 123-140
- ▼ A Needs-Based Change Strategy 126
- ▼ The Impact of Combined Action 129
- ▼ Learning from Combined Action 131

CHAPTER SEVEN
Nameless Change for Organizational Renewal ... 141-184
- ▼ Roles 144
- ▼ Stages of the Nameless Change Process 149
- ▼ Questions and Answers During Each Stage 163

CHAPTER EIGHT
Comparing the Models 185-199
- ▼ Strategic Comparison 186
- ▼ Tactical Comparison 189
- ▼ When to Use the Nameless Approach 195

APPENDIX
Collaborative Negotiation 200-211
- ▼ Preface 200
- ▼ Interest-Based Negotiation 204
- ▼ A Negotiation Primer for Combined Actions Teams 207
- ▼ The Payoff 211

BIBLIOGRAPHY 212-218
AUTHOR INDEX 219-220
SUBJECT INDEX 221-230

Words

It's only words...

The Bee Gees

Words inform, delineate, compel, and engage. They can also stereotype and objectify. It may be only words, but words are all it takes to categorize and name.

- Named change can become objectified change.
- Objectified change can become impersonal change.
- Impersonal change becomes ineffective change.

Who is changing? Who do we expect to change when we develop the plans and strategies we know will improve organizational performance?

- Is it employees?
- Is it people?
- Is it them?
- Is it us?

You may notice throughout this book that the word "employee" is used at certain times and the word "person" is used at others.

- Employees can be tallied and controlled.
- People need engagement and consideration.

The word "employee" is used when we're talking about the traditional model of change. The word "person" is used when we're discussing the nontraditional approach of nameless change. Hopefully, someday, people will be "people" and the objectification of both people and change will end.

Foreword

Frederick A. Miller
President and CEO, The Kaleel Jamison Consulting Group, Inc.

Frederick A. Miller has been a pioneer and practitioner of inclusive organizational change processes for more than 30 years. His clients have included some of the largest, most successful and most innovative organizations in the world, including Apple Computer, Dun & Bradstreet, Pillsbury-Grand Metropolitan, DuPont, GE Capital, Mobil, Ford Credit, Toyota Motor Sales, Freddie Mac, the Social Venture Network, the John D. and Catherine T. MacArthur Foundation, Los Alamos National Laboratories, and the City of San Diego. He serves on the Boards of Directors of Ben & Jerry's Homemade, Inc., the American Society for Training and Development (ASTD), Seton Health Systems, the Institute for Development Research, and The Living School. He is member and former board member of NTL Institute for Behavioral Science and the National Organization Development Network.

fred It's always an honor to be asked to write a foreword to someone's book. I feel especially proud to be associated with a book that challenges the conventional and often-flawed practice of organizational change.

Instead of going the conventional route and writing about my reactions to this book, I've decided to apply the book's basic premise to the creation of this foreword.

In the spirit of Glenn Allen-Meyer's *Nameless Organizational Change*, I'm not going to treat this foreword-writing assignment as a goal to be met, or an end-point to be reached, or a laundry-list box to be checked. I am going to *engage* in it as a process. As in Glenn's *Nameless* model, I'm going to …

Make it local.
Make it personal.
Make it customized and self-defining.
And make it interactive.

fred *So, Glenn, what do you think is the single most important point this book makes?*

glenn I would like readers to consider that change shouldn't be treated like a commodity to be marketed internally to people inside organizations. I'd like them to see that there are other ways to manage change— other ways that actually engage the wisdom and energy of the people who are being asked to change.

fred I agree. The lack of inclusion and engagement of people has, in my experience, been the single most destructive failing in organizations over the past 25 years. *Nameless Organizational Change* offers a strong rationale and model for addressing this. Although your unique work focuses on the processes of change implementation, this book is important in that it joins the growing body of material that is helping organizations make the transition from the Industrial Age to the Internet Age.

glenn My position has been that change is change, no matter what the age. There are right ways and wrong ways, and too many organizations have been doing it the wrong way. What you're saying has influenced my thoughts about the final manuscript. Could you say more about why these Internet times speak to the *Nameless Organizational Change* approach?

fred Obviously there are a lot of good things that have come out of the Industrial Revolution. It made things happen. It made *things*. Through mass production and mass marketing it made necessities into commodities. It made the tools of successful living and learning more available and affordable for everyone. But it also brought us hierarchy for the masses, not just for the military. It brought us "command-and-control" as a way of doing business and with it the treatment of people as merely hands and feet. "Just do your job, we're not paying you to think." The industrial-age organizational model of command-and-control assembly-line hierarchy also became the "standard" model of organizational change. It's one of those examples of conceptual tunnel-vision: if command-and-control is your vision of how organizations should be run, then command-and-control will be your vision of how organizations should be changed. So for the last 100 years or more, organizational change has usually meant, "change by executive fiat." If you were at one of the "hands-and-feet" levels of an organization, change was something that was done *to* you or *for* you.

But as you have shown in your book, that method of change does not fit the type of organizations that are emerging in this new century, and it clearly does not fit where we're going. One of the things I like about your model is the understanding that wisdom is not all at the top. The knowledge to fix the problems resides, at least in part, with the people who have the problems. Although others have said this before, you add value first by tracing the lineage and evolution of the "marketing paradigm" of change management, then by demonstrating how the unquestioned acceptance of this model limits voice and, therefore, limits the success of any given change effort.

To me and many others, this seems like common sense—people closest to the problem, working together with others who bring a perspective on change and problem solving, will obviously create the best solution.

glenn If it's so obvious, why is it not common?

fred That's a question for all humanity. Why isn't common sense more common? For organizations, I think the answer lies in the structure and management style of the Industrial Revolution. It was ruled from the top by the elite. It was an era of *elite* sense, not *common* sense. The influence of that era is still strong. I think this is one of the reasons for the name of your book. The self-importance of the fiat-driven change processes made it plain that they were pronouncements of the elite for the primary benefit of the elite, and that those who were expected to change were to behave like obedient hands and feet. The elite processes of corporate change, modeled after the core activities of marketing and accounting, make it easy to "sell" change to "employees" (notice the objectification of the term "employees") and to tally compliance. This is hardly a way to inspire motivation and commitment!

glenn Exactly! That's why I chose the title "Nameless Organizational Change." My experience is that the very first, and the very most damaging, exercise of control—elite control, as you put it—during change is experienced in that moment when the most senior leader thinks up or agrees to a catchy name or slogan for the change. Once the name is given, the wheels of marketing and control take over and the possibility of commitment is replaced by the certainty of compliance.

fred Commitment is riskier than compliance. Compliance can be tallied; commitment must be nurtured and treated as an investment. Investment in commitment is like investment in the stock market. It's risky. You have to work for it. You might have to give up something to get something. Investment in compliance is more of a "sure thing" with a "predictable" rate of return—one hundred managers with check marks next to "Supports the Change" on their performance appraisals really reassures senior leadership. The conservative low-return approach can be seen when managers are required to link all of their current activities to the goals and strategies of a corporate change program. If the current activities were working, there would be no need for change! Don't get conservative just when you need the returns the most!

glenn Fred, sometimes it feels as though I am swimming upriver on this.

fred The timing of your book is excellent, and you are swimming against the current of accepted change practice. You're not alone though. The Internet Age is teaching us things that support the model you are creating. I am choosing my words carefully here. I say it is teaching us, but I don't think we have learned much yet. I fully believe we are just at the beginning of a long and steep learning curve regarding living life and doing business in the age of the Internet. I hope through your book and the writings of others that the learning will continue and that things will be very different in the coming years.

glenn How specifically do you think the Internet Age is helping this come about?

fred Well, in one sense it's about speed, not just in production, but also speed of problem solving, speed of change. For organizations it's going to be about being nimble, getting the smartest and best people think-

Customized *Beginning of an era*

Internet → Speed → Getting close enough → 80% solution not perfect → can't wait for perfection

ing about something new or about different ways to do things. And because of this need for speed, it's about the need for getting close without having to be perfect—at least that is what is needed here in the beginning of this Internet Age.

This is very different from the era of Zero Defects, and the need for getting it right the first time, every time. This is more like the era of the 80 percent solution. Organizations and individuals can no longer wait to be certain. They have to act immediately, knowing they can't possibly have allowed for every variable, and plan for course adjustments that are certain to come. It's about customization. It's about a lot size of one—not the grand answer for all, not one-size-fits-all, and not the average common denominator. It's about the right solution, product, answer, action—for moments and situations that are fleeting and units that are less than the whole. It's acting today based on information and skills we know will change tomorrow. It's under the belief that customization brings about greater clarity of need, and in addressing those needs, you will get closer to a solution than any generalized approach. That is the essence of what I reflect on when I look at your model.

glenn

I'm confused, then. Do you think the "Nameless" model is new or just common sense?

fred

It's only new if you think common sense is new, which I don't happen to think. I think it is unpracticed. The essence of your model is the original intent of Deming and the quality movement. This is what continuous improvement was about. This was the intent of "work system redesign." The essence, the core, the original intent is to work closely with the people doing the work, to use their wisdom, to have them be more empowered and more involved in evolving/improving *their* processes. This is the essence you share. This is the common sense approach to organizational change that has been lost in the elite assumption that systemic change is driven by the power of those *farthest* from the work being done. Such waste is produced by this assumption!

What I see you doing in this book is continuing the advocacy of common sense:

• the common sense of Ken Blanchard and *The One-Minute Manager.*

• the common sense of Tom Peters' search for excellence, and his yelling at all of us that the key to success is talking to your people.

• the common sense of Rosabeth Moss Kanter and *The Tale of O.*

I think your point of view is a reaction that many share as a result of the "dumb" implementation of re-engineering and other half-thought-out fads of recent years.

There has been a very high and unnecessary cost for those efforts, and I think your book rightfully addresses some of that. I am glad that you are giving me the opportunity to be associated with such an effort. I definitely think you have something here worth writing about and telling people about.

We have to change the way that change has been implemented in organizations during the last 20 to 25 years. We have to get people to be involved in their own change process. We have to get leaders to be resources and coaches in the change process, not removed from such processes as aloof commanders-in-chief.

There's a certain irony in the "Nameless" process. Based on my experience over the past quarter-century, it is probably less expensive to implement change "locally" than through a glitzy global rollout, so I think there's a hidden financial benefit to what you're advocating. Local change can be much quicker, more effective and less disruptive, with greater buy-in at all levels. Global rollouts seem to be hangovers from the age of mass production; without local wisdom and implementation, they just beg for the delays and expense of unnecessary resistance, litigious backlash and "program of the month" cynicism.

glenn   Well, you've sold me on my own book!

fred   I congratulate you and thank you. Your book is a worthy and needed addition to the body of knowledge moving us into this new era and into the workplace and work-partnerships of the future. Your model is one that helps create organizations that allow people to bring their full selves to work. This full engagement of people's capabilities, of not just their hands and feet but their thinking and problem-solving abilities, is critical for organizations that want to stay competitive and especially for those that will thrive in the coming century. The key for them is to develop and retain talent, and to tap the wisdom of the people of the organization.

Thanks for the opportunity to engage in this dialogue with you. And now I'll write my traditional foreword...

The Traditional Foreword

This book is about the process of change—not only about the process of solving problems inside organizations, but also the change that is taking place in organizational structures around the globe. It's about the movement from the Industrial Age to the post-industrial age (which many of us are calling the Internet Age). This transition speaks to a diversity of humankind and the need for that diversity to be tapped, not only for public-relations window dressing and for reaching specialized markets, but for problem solving, innovation, and sustainable organizational SUCCESS.

This change speaks to the inclusion of the whole person into work life, not segmenting people like we segmented the production line during the Industrial Revolution.

The irony of the title of this book is that it speaks to this transitional moment in time in a manner that incorporates and embraces the uncertainty of what is to come:

- We are still not sure what to call this era (Post-Industrial? The Internet Age? The Information Age? The Communication Age? The Customization Age?)
- We can only partially see around the next corner.
- We all know there is a revolution afoot; we all feel it, and we all know the biggest impact is still ahead.

The Nameless model is a catalyst for change bigger than anything we've seen before, because if we bring together all these elements of the Nameless model:

- the diversity that is all around us and within us...
- and the values and practice of inclusion...
- and the engagement of the people closest to the problem in solving the problem...
- with the organization's leaders acting as coaches and resources...
- and a new world and frontier ahead of us...

...then no one can predict the outcome, or what it should be called, but we all know it offers greater potential than anything we've seen before in the history of organizations.

To Glenn, thanks for writing this book. To the reader, enjoy the journey.

Sincerely,

Frederick A. Miller
26 February, 2000

Introduction

The Hype of the Traditional Approach to Change

Change has gotten a bad name; just ask nearly any leader, middle manager, supervisor, or employee in even the most successful of organizations.

For the past five years I have been conducting an informal experiment with leaders and managers. Any time I find myself in front of a group where I am expected to discuss change, I lead a free association on the word.

I say "change," you say...

The two most frequent words I hear in response: "resist" and "pain." Ouch.

In my organization development practice, I have been asked by countless leaders and executives to assist in the implementation of change. I have been asked to be a salesperson of change. I have used every tool imaginable to fulfill my responsibilities as a change agent—from encounter groups to reengineering, training to future search, total quality to open space technology, self-directed work teams to collaborative organizational design—and people continue to generate negative associations with change. At some point, I took note of my growing sense of disillusion.

I have found myself in the midst of the most aggressively programmed organizational cultures. I have seen changes choreographed with the precision of Broadway performances with all managers and employees in their places awaiting direction. At various times, I have found myself being asked to serve as the assistant director of such performances, making sure everyone understood the steps and hit their marks on time. Over time, I grew less comfortable with this role, wondering why, if changes were so valuable, did they have to be implemented in this manner?

Rather than quit my practice, I became a student of the game, learning not only how organizations conceive of and implement change, but also how people find ways to resist change even when they know that resistance, in the words of a popular science fiction show, "is futile."

In most large organizations, resistance to change poses difficult challenges. Leaders expend tremendous time, energy, clout, and resources trying to make change the way change has been made in the past, with extensive training programs and complicated competency-driven performance management plans, procedures, and policies offering some sense of certainty to executives who hope the return-on-investment to change will prove worthwhile. Over time, these accepted change methodologies have become bureaucratized with complex organizational structures established to transform executive goals into "tangible," justifiable results. While there are many different approaches to, and infrastructures of, change, nearly all share important similarities illustrated in Figure 1.

Traditionally, the executive of an organization (or the most senior individual or group) sponsors a change. Ideally, this person or group targets the change to the results of a careful analysis of the organization, its environment, and the gaps between the two. The result of the executive's work is usually a named project with a vision, goals, time-frame, and general allocation of resources.

Because the executive does not administer the change, s/he turns administrative responsibility over to a leadership team or task force charged with creating a detailed project plan, assigning accountabilities, budgeting resources, and establishing a plan to monitor progress. If this team has authority, it can then hold others accountable for implementation of the change. If it does not, then it presents a proposed strategic plan to the executive who ratifies it and sponsors its implementation in all targeted areas.

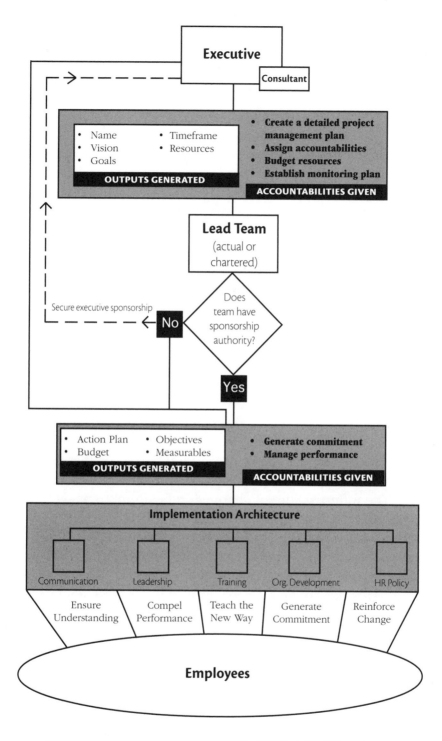

FIGURE ONE: THE TRADITIONAL APPROACH TO CHANGE

The human resource functions of communication, training, and organization development are used to drive the desired change outward into the organization. Communication specialists ensure understanding, training specialists teach the new way to everyone expected to change, and organization development professionals use a variety of techniques to build participation and commitment. HR policy can be altered to reinforce behaviors consistent with the change. Leaders are briefed on the change and are given performance management tools they will use to hold others accountable for behaviors consistent with the change.

Often with great hype, this entire infrastructure is activated to ensure that others change. Those "others"—middle managers and employees—are by now quite familiar with the process. They understand what they must do to be in compliance. Usually they comply and the change is made.

Leaders and executives, confident in the technical beauty of the process, accept compliance as evidence of a successful change and move on. Those asked to change then go through the change-aggravated experiences that leave them saying "pain" when I say "change."

The infrastructure of change is a beautiful thing—for a simpler time when people in organizations did what they were told and when competitive pressures and limited information forced few changes. In today's dynamic world, the process can be cumbersome, expensive, inefficient, and error-ridden. And, since it is used to "change others," it is also flawed. Its flaw comes from the typical human dynamics generated when one person or group attempts to change another.

Like dancers in a show, employees continue to smile during change. Yes, they may gripe a bit, but they tend to perform well. We believe they change until we consider the hidden costs of resistance and stress produced by the typical model of organizational change.

This book also offers a new approach: the nameless approach, the simplified form of which can be viewed in Figure 2.

The nameless approach to change offers a new, yet proven, series of actions leaders and change agents can take to improve their organizations without the resistance usually associated with organizational change. The approach is "nameless" for two reasons:

First, during change, your organization's constituents and stakeholders should focus their attention on the improvements being made, not on the program being followed. Second, in today's climate of continuous change, people at work are more than ready to cynically rename the most ambitious change programs. Use of the nameless approach allows you to reap the gains of change without all of the pain associated with the "name game's" hype, hammer, and hope.

UNDERSTANDING NAMELESS CHANGE

Although the balance of this book will help you better understand the need for, and principles of, the nameless change model, a few points here will orient you to the approach:

Why the name "nameless change?"

The approach is called "nameless" to remind leaders and change agents that change can be implemented without first being named and treated as something to be marketed to managers and employees. The model is designed to stay in the background during organizational transformation to avoid the negative reactions often produced by the programmatic implementation of named approaches such as Total Quality, Reengineering, and Teams.

Nameless change is an attempt to help today's leaders and change agents see change with fresh eyes. We've become too familiar with change and our assumptions often cloud our vision. The assumptions of the nameless change model will help you see change as a process rather than as a thing, and the human reaction to programmed change as a symptom instead of a disposition.

What is nameless change?
In this approach, groups of supervisors and change agents disperse into the organization in a combined action team using the goals, tools, and processes of a change to help people at the frontline of the work being done solve real-time operational issues. Where alignment between the change and operational issues is not obvious, the combined action team uses negotiation techniques to blend the goals of the change with frontline issues. This blending creates the momentum that propels the change.

Why is nameless change needed?
Today's leaders and managers express frustration at the pace of change. Leaders who have to explain the merits of today's changes may find themselves explaining or marketing contrary merits for tomorrow's. This repetition renders marketing inefficient as a way to generate change in organizations facing dynamic, turbulent environments.

How do you sell a change that has no name?
You don't. Using the nameless change model, you help people in your organization *use*, to their advantage, the tools and principles of the change your organization needs to make. This model provides an architecture for the self-selling of the merits of the change. In this way, a tremendous burden is lifted from the shoulders of leaders and managers who would prefer to spend time making needed

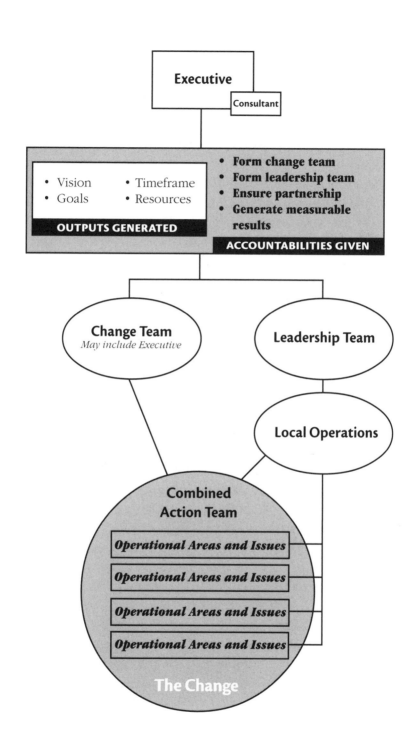

FIGURE 2: THE NAMELESS APPROACH

improvements with people instead of selling changes to employees.

How do people react to the nameless change process?

The same way they do when anyone listens to understand and then lends assistance to help *them* solve *their* problem. They express a gratitude that translates into the motivation and commitment that propels the change.

How new is this model?

Ancient in the sense that people have always been motivated by whatever they need to do to improve their ability to do their job, solve their problems, or reach their goals. As a complete architecture for change, the model is new.

The nameless approach shares many early-stage similarities with the traditional model. Executives still define the change and hold others accountable for achieving success. The major differences between the approaches are found under the level of the executive. In the nameless approach, a team of change agents partners with local operations and makes the change at the intersection of the goals of the change and the needs and issues on the front line. Change starts inside *Combined Action Teams* of change agents and local personnel. While this may not seem groundbreaking, no model for organizational change offers an architecture specifically designed to blend the goals of a change with the real-time reality of people at the frontline of work. Don't be deceived by the simplicity of the model at this stage of presentation. Decades of experience leave today's leaders and change agents with pervasive assumptions about change. The acceptance of these assumptions converts simple truths about who we are and how we change into counter-intuitive complexities ignored during the dance of change.

The Hope of *Nameless Organizational Change*

The themes presented on the pages that follow are broad, as they must be to state the need for a new approach to change. The hope for this book is that the reader will find it interesting, challenging, eye-opening, enjoyable and, most of all, inspirational. It was written to support anyone who hopes leaders, managers, and employees alike will generate newer, more hopeful and uplifting associations with the word "change."

For Whom Was This Book Written?

This book was written for leaders, managers, and change agents hoping to implement the next change more smoothly, completely, and harmoniously than the last. Inside, you will find unique ideas to consider and actions to take. You may even uncover surprisingly obvious answers to your questions about the benefits and limitations of current paradigms of organizational change. This book was also written to provide researchers, scholars, and educators with challenging concepts to examine, evaluate, and, where appropriate, disseminate.

How to Use This Book

If you are primarily interested in getting a quick sense of the nameless change model, you can jump to Chapters Six, Seven, and Eight. They will help you understand the source of the model, and will give you a sense of how the nameless change architecture operates. Chapters Two through Five will help you understand why such a model is needed in today's turbulent environment. If you plan to use the nameless change model, please have respect for the resistance you may encounter from others operating within the traditional paradigm of programmatic change. The early chapters will help you address such resistance.

Overall, the book is organized as follows:

Chapter One describes the most usual *Current Assumptions About Organizational Change.*

Chapter Two, *Everyday Stress in Organizations,* outlines the basic level of stress present in organizations as a result of the simple act of gathering individuals to do, or produce, something in common together. This baseline level of stress is exacerbated by change.

Chapter Three, *Programmatic Methods of Change*, provides an overview of the most typical methods of change and describes how change has become a commodity that is internally marketed to employees. The marketing of change is a significant cause of resistance to change.

Chapter Four, *Resistance to Programmatic Change*, illuminates the human dynamics underlying resistance to, and stress from, the traditional approach to organizational change.

Chapter Five, *The Bottom-Line Costs of Resistance*, tallies the cost of employee resistance and stress. Knowing the bottom line impact of the traditional approach to change will help leaders and executives consider a new way.

Chapter Six, *Finding a New Way to Change*, helps us locate a benchmarked example of a better way to make change.

Chapter Seven, *Nameless Change for Organizational Renewal*, highlights the model's roles and stages and offers answers to common questions about it.

Chapter Eight, *Comparing the Models*, offers a final comparison of the nameless and programmatic approaches to change along with guidelines for when to use, and when not to use, nameless change.

It is not the relative value of the work that determines the value of the name, but the institutionalized value of the title that can be used as a means of defending or maintaining the value of the work.

Pierre Bourdieu

They set you on the treadmill and they made you change your name.

Bernie Taupin

Current Assumptions About Organizational Change

A culture that knows how to land a person on the moon and bring him safely back to earth knows how to initiate and complete projects. Unfortunately, the project-oriented, programmatic nature of today's methods of organizational change turn the process of change into a tangible thing that can be implemented—and resisted. Our assumptions about the nature of change act as a force that guides our behavior. Like gravity acting upon a rolling snowball, our assumptions lead to outcomes that gain strength and momentum as they roll through our organizations. Many of these outcomes limit the effectiveness of the changes we hope to implement.

The visionary leadership of President Kennedy marshaled the resources of a nation to get behind the race to the moon. Like Kennedy, the leaders of today's largest organizations know how to generate momentum toward a goal. With the secrecy of a Manhattan Project, leaders gather to identify strategic strengths and areas of opportunity for their organization. Out of such analyses, they identify goals to be reached and specific steps to be taken to get there. Then, like Kennedy, they use the visionary potential of their position to announce the changes needed to reach the goal. Supported by entire organizational infrastructures, they can be certain the change will be disseminated throughout the organization in a series of big announcement events, training programs, briefings, and brown bag lunches. Video tapes, music, buttons, banners, and coffee mugs emblazoned with the name of the change reach out to all managers and employees with the message of change. This is the programmatic approach to organizational change.

While the programmatic approach does help an organization achieve economies of scale with respect to the number of employees reached with the imperative for change, it is a strategy that is useful mostly during times of relative stability. When change becomes frequent and an organization is forced to reinvent itself on a regular basis, the programmatic approach can become unwieldy. The programmatic approach is a standardized, rule-bound, authority and accountability-driven model for the implementation of major change. As such, it is a poor adaptation to times of continuous change. The result of the lack of fit between the demands for continuous change and an organization's default use of the programmatic approach can be observed in the cynicism, stress, and resistance expressed by people in organizations undergoing programmatic change.

Lands' End, a premier mail-order retailer of clothing and home furnishings, was lauded in Levering and Moskowitz's 1993 *The 100 Best Companies to Work for in America*. In early 1993, programmatic efforts to implement "modern" management ideas caused a level of internal resistance so steep that the CEO brought in to make the changes was replaced after barely two years on the job. The homespun, laid-back culture at Lands' End's Dodgeville, Wisconsin. headquarters had become a source of pride for

Land's End employees. A review of the situation at the company indicates that resistance to the change grew out of the ways in which the changes were implemented (see "Bad Fit," *The Wall Street Journal*, Monday, April 3, 1995). Programs and practices with mandated participation were resented by people who had never experienced such an approach to change. A new mission statement reading, "Turn every customer into a friend by delivering quality products, honest value and world class service," was "displayed on company bulletin boards, buttons and banners overhanging [Lands' End's] cavernous warehouse." One person summed up the reaction by saying, "We don't need anything hanging over our heads telling us to do something we're already doing."

In response to his termination, the CEO, William T. End (no relation to the company name) said, "The big issue we're talking about here is change and people's ability to adapt to it." Of the Board Chairman who removed him, End said, "[Mr. Comer]...saw change as a threat to the organization."

Many of today's most successful leaders are mystified by the negative reaction of their workforces to the changes they try to implement in a programmatic manner. "After all," they may assert, "we made changes the exact same way in the 1980's. Why is this workforce, today, so resistant?"

When people at work grow tired of the slogans, training programs, and accountabilities that don't seem to add value to the work being done on the line, it is not the changes they dislike—it is the way the changes are implemented.

An initial step toward significantly enhancing organizational performance might be made by evaluating a few current assumptions about change and accepting the implications of acting on those assumptions.

ASSUMPTION #1:

Change Has Become Its Own Domain

Like the ubiquitous *.com* and *.org* Internet domains, change has become part of the popular lexicon. When a fast food chain like Taco Bell runs a major media campaign with the slogan, "Change is Good," we can be sure that the phrase is really an affirmation for people who feel that change is often rather unpleasant. The domain of change reaches into everyone's lives. In our organizations, leaders, managers and employees alike feel its omnipresence and wish its impact would diminish. Instead of simply assuming, "Well, people just don't like change," the leaders of today's organizations would do better to step back and look at change much like an infant examines the patterns of light and dark streaming through a window. To adults, it's just light. To someone who has never seen it before, it is full of possibility. Who sees greater detail in such a phenomenon? Clearly one who sees it with the mind of a beginner. We think we know change because we are so used to it.

When we observe change with fresh eyes, we cannot help but notice that change is neither a place, nor a domain, nor a commodity, nor a thing. Change is merely a name we give to a complex process by which people exchange one set of assumptions and expectations for another.

Or, it is the name we give to something we think people dislike.

ASSUMPTION #2:

Change Has to Be Marketed to Employees

Because change has become so omnipresent, the leaders of today's organizations, with the help of consultants, have hit upon a change implementation strategy that appears to work time and time again: determine the change to be made, give the change a name, market the change to the organization, secure employee "buy-in," train all who need to be trained, then quantify and pronounce tangible improvements. This architecture of change supports the marketing of change. From the use of consultants, to reliance on the human resource functions of training and organization development, to the application of performance management schemes, the marketing model holds sway. The entire process starts with the conversion of the complex adjustments in skills, relationships, structures, and processes that form the core of any true change, to a named "thing" that can be promoted and monitored throughout an organization.

ASSUMPTION #3:

Managers and leaders are the salespeople of change

Decades ago, in less turbulent times, an organization could change by fiat. Henry Ford did not need the buy-in of the managers below him to set the corporate strategy of "any color Model T you like—as long as it's black." Through the years, changes in the expectations of people at work, and in leadership styles, have necessitated a softer approach on the part of those who wish to set strategy or implement change.

In the Sixties and Seventies, leaders were told that to get work done, or to change the way work was done, they needed employees to participate in decision making processes that would impact their working lives. In the Eighties and Nineties, such participation has been accomplished on teams with levels of autonomy that would have shocked Mr. Ford. Such teams, it is thought, will be able to act quickly to make changes in response to needs discovered at the level of customer contact. Their autonomy also makes them more difficult to command and control.

The leaders of today's organizations find themselves responding equally as quickly to the uncertain conditions found in markets and environments characterized by nearly continuous change and upheaval. Unfortunately, today's leaders do not have the same tools of control at their disposal as did Henry Ford. In today's organizations, they know they must "market" their change visions to their organizations through programmatic interventions that have a great deal in common with the mass marketing campaigns they use to persuade consumer purchasing in the marketplace.

The demands for adjustment and improvement have become so omnipresent that change is no longer treated as a process that can carefully and completely wind its way through an organization. Now, an organization's change program is a "product" each and every leader is expected to sell to his or her employees. We should not be surprised, then, to find that today's leaders express concern over having to sell one change to employees in one quarter and another, often conflicting, change during the next.

ASSUMPTION #4:

Employees Will "Buy" Into Change

Leaders typically assume that the persuasiveness of the business case for change will generate enough employee buy-in to allow the change to move forward in a timely manner. As the Land's End case illustrates, however, there is often an inverse relationship between the glitz of the change program and the support of the organizations's people. Leaders tend to act as if people at work are truly independent consumers in the marketplace of the "purchase" of change. They are not. While a consumer may walk away from the purchase of one home in favor of another, people at work are not so free to walk away from the choices offered by their organization. To leaders, employee buy-in to change is the single, sole, purpose of persuasive, programmatic change efforts. From within this paradigm, resistance to change is simply an unsightly adjunct to change that can be eliminated through accountabilities or attrition.

People at work, for their part, are presumed to be buyers of what leaders have to sell—buyers with the same freedom of choice in the organization that they have in the open market for goods and services outside of work.

ASSUMPTION #5:

Compliance is Necessary and Beneficial

In a truly free market, choice minimizes resistance. The reality of choice looks very different inside organizations depending especially upon one's perspective. To a person with nomimal skills in a tight labor market, or to a skilled professional with teenage children in school, choice is more of an illusion than it might be to the mobile nomads of today's corporate leadership class. People who do not have great latitude for choice may comply with a change—at least externally.

Lack of perceived choice produces resistance and stress. When the stress is externalized, it causes resistance that can be seen in people who actively fight the change. When it is internalized, it can cause health and performance problems that may not even be recognized as being related to the change.

While resistance and stress might not bring an organization's change to a complete halt, these reactions can do much worse—they can eat its efficiency from the inside out without anyone recognizing that the expanding timetables, illnesses, accidents, absenteeisms, and turnover are related to the methods used to implement the change. Compliance—the facade of cooperation and commitment—is a dangerous by-product of programmatic change.

ASSUMPTION #6:
This is the Right Way to Change

Decades of scholarly research and practical experience have helped today's leaders know what to do when change is needed. The principles and practices of change have become so well-honed that it would be ludicrous to expect leaders to do anything differently. Yet, expect we must. Unfortunately, models offering ways to change more appropriate to the times are destined to swim upstream against the tide of current practice.

UNDERSTANDING THE RESULTS

Our assumptions determine the results we get. There is an axiom in the field of education that goes like this: *Our students will perform as we expect them to perform.* Experiments prove this out. A teacher who is told she is teaching a class of "marginal performers" will end up with students who perform marginally in comparison with students in classes whose teachers who were told nothing. Better still is the performance of students whose teachers are led to believe they are teaching "superb performers." While the teachers with biased assumptions may do nothing deliberately to teach their students differently than teachers who are told nothing, their behaviors are clouded by their perceptions and the results turn out to be rather predictable (for a review of related studies, see Rosenthal & Rubin, 1978).

Similarly, the assumptions we hold about the nature of change determine the results we see during change.

▼ If we treat change as a "thing," people will see it as such and will decide, often on face value, whether it is a good thing or a bad thing.

▼ If we treat change as a commodity to be marketed, then people at work will respond as they do to items marketed to them in the free economy—they may "drive past the billboard" without even taking notice, they may inquire, or they might "change the channel" and avoid the pronouncements altogether. Worse yet, they may recognize the difference between their ability to make their own purchase decisions outside of work and the more circumscribed choice they have while at work. This awareness leads to cynicism and resistance.

▼ When we assume that our leaders will effectively sell, and re-sell, change to employees, we run the risk of creating cynical people at all levels of the organization who question their own integrity.

▼   If we assume that we are successful when employees comply with the mandates of change, then we are likely to see only two options during change: people either comply or they resist. We miss the fact that while all of us are quite capable of doing things we don't really want to do, doing so often creates a level of discomfort or stress that sneaks out in illnesses, accidents, loss of motivation, or the decision to leave and move on to another company. The either/or paradigms of marketing and compliance blind us to the gray areas of the dynamics of organizational change. The gray areas drain the efficiencies of the changes we make.

Figure 1.1, The Snowball Model, serves as a visual representation of the way in which the basic level of stress present in any organization builds, through change, like a snowball rolling downhill toward a wall. And, like the snowball, stress and resistance hit the wall in our organizations with an impact that shatters the full potential of change. The zone of impact is a place where stress and resistance are converted into costs that drain the efficiency of, and returns from, change.

▼   Lastly, if we assume that the current paradigms telling us how to change are absolutely correct, then we may pass over the opportunity to review another model that may be appropriate for the continuing times of continuous change.

The following chapters follow the snowball of change downhill, diverting it before impact with a new way to change.

The Snowball Model

Organizational Performance in the Context of Change

Work

Change

Resistance

The Zone of
PRODUCTION

The Zone of
IMPROVEMENT

The Zone of
REACTION

• *Division of Labor* • *Scientific Management* • *Management-by-Objectives* • *Bureaucracy* • *Work Processes* • *Span of Control*	• *Problem-Solving* • *Internal Marketing*	• *Task Forces* • *Implementation Teams* • *Performance Management* • *Training*
Basic structures, processes, and activities support production and performance—they also cause a baseline level of stress in individuals that is managed through a variety of means.	*Competitive pressures create demand for change. Problem-solving techniques are used to generate a plan for change. Internal marketing approaches implement changes throughout the organization.*	*Change sponsors use participatory techniques in planning and implementation stages to control counter-productive reactions to change. Hard- and soft-skills training prepares the organization for change, and performance management processes ensure compliance.*

THE SNOWBALL MODEL:

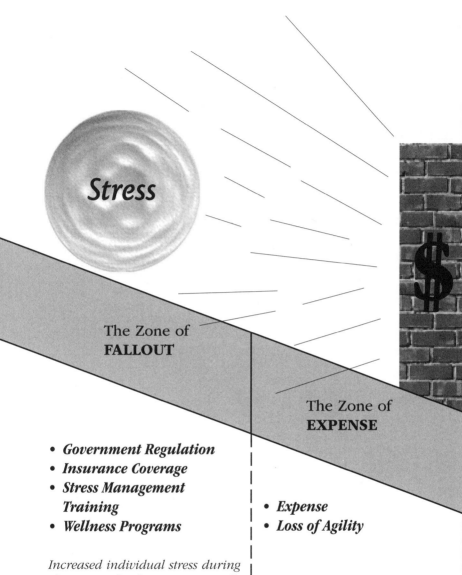

Stress

The Zone of
FALLOUT

The Zone of
EXPENSE

- *Government Regulation*
- *Insurance Coverage*
- *Stress Management*
  Training
- *Wellness Programs*

- *Expense*
- *Loss of Agility*

Increased individual stress during change can lead to increases in illness, accident, substance abuse, absenteeism, tardiness, and turnover rates. Leaders sponsor stress management, safety, and wellness programs to stem the fallout from change.

Fallout slows the change and adds expense. Costs diminish the effectiveness of the change and leave the organization less well-equipped to implement future changes.

ORGANIZATIONAL PERFORMANCE IN THE CONTEXT OF CHANGE

2

Everyday Stress
in Organizations

*Before organizations change, they produce. Before we
can understand a new approach to change, we must
understand the factors that lead to the inefficiency of
so many organizational change programs and accepted change methodologies. To better understand
these factors, we must first examine the culture of work
and the adaptive traits developed by humans during
roughly three million years of evolution. The nature
of organizing creates a baseline level of stress in people
at work—stress that acts as a kernel around which
the additional stressors of change congeal.*

The urge to work is nearly universal, as is the urge to
create organizations capable of channeling work energy into desired products and services. Whether we work
to survive, to accumulate wealth, or to give expression to
our inner passion and creativity, work is as much a part of
human life as the drawing of breath.

Stephen Hawking, the brilliant cosmologist stricken and
immobilized by ALS (Lou Gehrig's disease), has continued
to provide leading-edge thought in his field by utilizing
technology that helps him to write and speak by selecting
letters with puffs of breath; yet the thought of so complete
an immobilization would frighten most. Further evidence
for the fear of inactivity was described in the April 7, 1999

issue of *USA Today* in a story entitled "Big Apple Abuzz Over Blaine Burial" which described illusionist David Blaine's effort to break the record for the longest time buried alive. Blaine had himself placed in a clear plastic "coffin" in a Plexiglas tank filled with two tons of water. Blaine's collaborator said the stunt fascinated because it involved four situations people fear:

▼ being in a confined space
▼ not eating
▼ being in an inescapable situation
▼ having no privacy

Some may draw parallels between these fears and the complaints people express about working in certain modern workplaces. In fact, the parallel is not completely misguided. Organizational structures do, in fact, limit individual behavior to a certain degree to ensure unified effort. The efficiency and effectiveness of such structuring is the product of centuries of evolution of the concepts of both the individual and the organization.

As societies developed and humans learned to increase productivity beyond what was required to feed and house themselves, attention turned to surplus—and to wealth. As early as 1491 B.C., when Moses was urged to lead the people of Israel via delegated authority, we learned to create the best possible organizations for the optimization of human effort. The structures, processes, and technologies of today's organizations are, in themselves, as wondrous as the products and services they make possible. And yet, anyone who has worked knows that they are imperfect structures for the expression of human emotion and creativity and for the development of well-rounded, fully realized individuals. While organizations do not exist for this purpose, we must acknowledge that in Western society in general, and in the United States in particular, individuals increasingly expect a degree of liberty and self-expression in their lives and, to a certain extent, in their jobs. The difference between organizations and the needs and desires of the people who work within them can be seen as a source of baseline stress found in today's organizations.

THE ORGANIZATIONAL MONOCULTURE

A drive up Florida's Turnpike from Miami to Orlando ultimately brings one to Florida's Indian River region—the "fruit basket." Indian River fruit signs are ubiquitous in Florida, and fruit from this area fills supermarket produce sections across the nation. For twenty miles, from horizon to horizon on both sides of the Turnpike, a driver experiences the trance-inducing passing of row upon row of citrus trees, many of which are tall and squared off like green orange juice cartons turned upside-down. This vast citrus farm is an ecological monoculture—an area where nearly every other plant variety has been carefully eliminated to facilitate the efficient production of a single type of crop. On a map the region is highlighted with light blue icons indicating swampland—one of the most diverse ecosystems on the planet. What was once swampland, however, is now drained by orderly canals that divert the water's flow for irrigation. The trees appear to be stupendously healthy, which they must be to yield a world's bounty of oranges and grapefruits. It is not the crop that is stressed—it is the plants and animals displaced by the citrus. Entire pyramids of interrelated natural systems are no longer present in this region.

Like the Indian River region, workplaces are monocultures, with an organization's various departments and divisions existing as but variegated forms of a single species designed to accomplish a shared goal. When it comes to the existence of divergent varieties, organization by product, by function, by region, by customer, or by matrix is as unimportant as would be the placement of hundreds of square miles of citrus trees in rows, squares, circles, mouse ears, or fractal patterns. The reality is that some varieties are "in" while many other varieties are clearly "out."

FOR NOT EVEN FOR A MOMENT CAN A MAN BE WITHOUT ACTION. HELPLESSLY ARE ALL DRIVEN TO ACTION BY THE FORCES BORN OF NATURE.

—*Bhagavad Gita*

LIVING TO WORK

In organizations, the desired varieties include professionalism, respect for authority, discipline, subordinating one's goals to another's, specialization, and (somewhat under the surface—the tubers of workplace monoculture) making your boss look good, self protection, and "talking a good game." Less-desired varieties include dreaming, family, balance, poetry, transcendence, individualism, and artistry. If only these less-desired varieties of human behavior could be eradicated as quickly and as completely as an apple tree in a citrus grove.

As we know, they cannot; nor would we truly wish them banished from our organizations. But most large organizations demand certain behaviors and either ignore, or overtly or covertly prohibit, certain others. Fortunately, most human adults are resilient enough to compartmentalize their lives by expressing certain parts of themselves at work and certain other parts outside of work. Some people do this with ease; others struggle. The existence of the occasional "struggler" indicates that compartmentalization is not a completely stress-free response. In fact, even the most proficient organizational man or woman experiences times at work when they must "bite their tongue," "swallow their pride," or just "cool out" for a while—such is the nature of the organizational monoculture.

All organizations demand certain behaviors and prohibit others. A night watchman at a power generation facility might wish to nap, but he knows he cannot. Or, witness the work of a form stamper in a plastics firm. While the heat and repetition may be stressful, she understands that such conditions are to be tolerated for the sake of a paycheck and, perhaps, job satisfaction. Consider the discomfort experienced by a musician-turned-manager who has to table a creative idea because her boss makes it clear that it would be too expensive to implement.

We experience stress at work as a part of the normal activities of production. Most of us find these levels tolerable; some of us experience a degree of debilitation caused by a poor fit with the organizational monoculture. The existence of a baseline level of stress in any worker's experience within an organization is a function of the tightness of the fit between the goals, needs, and drives of the individual and the goals, needs, purposes, and activities of

> THE FRENCH PHILOSOPHER HENRI BERGSON JUSTLY POINTED OUT THAT IT WOULD BE MORE APPROPRIATE TO CALL OUR SPECIES HOMO FABER (THE MAKING MAN) THAN HOMO SAPIENS (THE KNOWING MAN), FOR THE CHARACTERISTIC FEATURE OF MAN IS NOT HIS WISDOM BUT HIS CONSTANT URGE TO WORK ON IMPROVING HIS ENVIRONMENT AND HIMSELF.
>
> —Hans Selye

THE WORKING SPECIES

Any man who has stood at twelve o'clock at the single narrow doorway, which serves as the place of exit for the hands employed in the great cotton-mills, must acknowledge, that an uglier set of men and women, of boys and girls, taking them in mass, it would be impossible to congregate in a smaller compass. Their complexion is sallow and pallid—with a peculiar flatness of feature, caused by the want of a proper quantity of adipose substance to cushion out the cheeks. Their stature low—the average height of four hundred men, measured at different times, and different places, being five feet six inches. Their limbs slender, and playing badly and ungracefully. A very general bowing of the legs. Great numbers of girls and women walking lamely or awkwardly, with raised chests and spinal flexures. Nearly all have flat feet, accompanied with a down-tread, differing very widely from the elasticity of action in the foot and ankle, attendant upon perfect formation. Hair thin and straight many of the men having but little beard, and that in patches of a few hairs, much resembling its growth among the red men of America. A spiritless and dejected air, a sprawling and wide action of the legs, and an appearance, taken as a whole, giving the world but "little assurance of a man," or if so, "most sadly cheated of his fair proportions…" (Gaskell, 1833).

WORKING AS A THREAT TO LIFE

the organization. In the following chapters, we explore specific stressors faced by workers in times of turbulent change and acknowledge the reality of a baseline level of stress in today's workplaces—a level that is increasing as organizations strive continually to optimize the efficiency of the processes of production.

While no one could rightly claim that work in today's modern corporate organization is more stressful than, say, the labor of a seventeenth-century foundry worker, we might say that a significant proportion of the stress one experiences at work stems from the difference between one's *expectations* for working life and the reality found at work. No one would argue about the debilitating conditions in a seventeenth-century foundry, but we must also remember that our hypothetical employee of that period *expected* such conditions and perhaps drew consolation from a belief in the redemptive nature of suffering in this life for a reward in the next for obedience to lord, master, and Church. While the physical conditions of such work severely endangered health and limited the span of life, there was not a general sense that "Everyone else has liberty, so why should not I?" Emotional stress of the type described in this book is produced when one recognizes a threat to some aspect of self, and the body, quite on its own, mounts a response. When the particulars of one's life are indistinguishable from the background of every other life, then no threat is perceived, much as prey cannot distinguish the pattern of a leopard from the background of grassland. Stress is an emotional reaction to the conditions of work that leads to either active resistance or passive resistance (unwilling compliance, withdrawal, or internalization of emotion resulting in a "slow burn" of body and mind over time). To develop these types of stress and resistance, one must have a reference point of opportunity outside of one's own life upon which to fix attention. By

▼ As of tomorrow, employees will only be able to access the building using individual security cards. Pictures will be taken next Wednesday and employees will receive their cards in two weeks.

▼ What I need is a list of specific unknown problems we will encounter.

▼ E-mail is not to be used to pass on information or data. It should be used only for company business.

▼ This project is so important, we can't let things that are more important interfere with it.

▼ Doing it right is no excuse for not meeting the schedule. No one will believe you solved this problem in one day! We've been working on it for months. Now, go act busy for a few weeks and I'll let you know when it's time to tell them.

▼ My boss spent the entire weekend retyping a 25-page proposal that only needed corrections. She claims the disk I gave her was damaged and she couldn't edit it. The disk I gave her was write-protected.

▼ Quote from the boss: "Teamwork is a lot of people doing what 'I' say."

▼ My sister passed away and her funeral was scheduled for Monday. When I told my boss, he said she died so that I would have to miss work on the busiest day of the year. He then asked if we could change her burial to Friday. He said, "That would be better for me."

▼ We recently received a memo from senior management saying, "This is to inform you that a memo will be issued today regarding the subject mentioned above."

TABLE 2.1: QUOTES CONTEST (INSPIRED BY DILBERT)

▼ This gem is the closing paragraph of a nationally-circulated memo from a large communications company: "Lucent Technologies is endeavorily determined to promote constant attention on current procedures of transacting business focusing emphasis on innovative ways to better, if not supersede, the expectations of quality!"

▼ We know that communication is a problem, but the company is not going to discuss it with the employees.

▼ One day my boss asked me to submit a status report to him concerning a project I was working on. I asked him if tomorrow would be soon enough. He said, "If I wanted it tomorrow, I would have waited until tomorrow to ask for it!"

▼ As director of communications, I was asked to prepare a memo reviewing our company's training programs and materials. In the body of the memo one of the sentences mentioned the "pedagogical approach" used by one of the training manuals. The day after I routed the memo to the executive committee, I was called into the HR Director's office, and was told that the executive VP wanted me out of the building by lunch. When I asked why, I was told that she wouldn't stand for "perverts" (pedophiles?) working in her company. Finally he showed me her copy of the memo, with her demand that I be fired, with the word "pedagogical" circled in red. The HR Manager was fairly reasonable, and once he looked the word up in his dictionary and made a copy of the definition to send to my boss, he told me not to worry. He would take care of it. Two days later a memo to the entire staff came out, directing us that no words which could not be found in the local Sunday newspaper could be used in company memos. A month later, I resigned. In accordance with company policy, I created my resignation letter by pasting words together from the Sunday paper.

contrast, then, everyday life looks like something to change—something to either run away from or to fight. Today, an person merely has to turn on the television to see the full opportunity afforded those with fame, money, and power and the stark differences between those "at the top" and those in the middle or at the bottom. Anyone who has ever been subjected to the frequently whimsical nature of leadership and authority understands full well the difference between social liberty and organizational liberty. Consider the humor and frustration at the core of the true stories collected for a contest inspired by the cartoon strip, *Dilbert*, circulated on the Internet, and presented here in Table 2.1.

A Brief History of Work

Why is the Dilbert cartoon strip so popular today? Perhaps it is because the gap between the drives and expectations of individuals and the structures and strictures of organizations has never been so wide. Table 2.2 (a-e) traces the development of this gap through the ages.

From the writings of Plato in the third century B.C. to the revelations of Martin Luther in the sixteenth century, individuals, for the most part, believed themselves to be subject to the will of others with greater knowledge, anointment, or position. Even the democratizing principles of the early Christian movement became institutionalized in a Catholic Church dogma forbidding the acquisition of knowledge and the pursuit of happiness in this life as sinful rejections of the one true reality of the afterlife. For two thousand years, the population of the Western world was predestined for obedience to external forces—philosopher, pope, aristocrat, owner of capital, holder of information. We might even call the years between Plato and the Magna Carta "The Age of the Fatalistic Group," for during this time, people saw themselves as members of distinct, impermeable classes codified by the higher law or Word of God as interpreted by philosophers, first, then priests, later. What we now know as Western society has been tailor-made for the imposition of a labor-intensive, class-reinforcing form of industry. This form expressed its zenith in the feudal structures found during the Middle Ages when serfs and vassals worked for the right to live on land owned by the King and administered by an aristocratic "middle class."

It was not until the Magna Carta that Western culture experienced a call for the realignment of rights within the social structure. This change, however, was not expressed as a demand for *individual* rights. The Magna Carta called for the enforcement of rights for the aristocratic *class* of people. The period of time from the Magna Carta, in 1215, to the seventeenth-century writings of Thomas Hobbes can be identified, for our purposes, as "The Age of The Empowered Group" for it was during this time that people advocated, *as a class,* for the rights of all members of that class. Saint Thomas Aquinas and Martin Luther, each in their own ways, broke the yoke of fatalism that had kept groups in alignments of subservience. Should it come as any surprise, then, to find that the empowerment of groups presages the ages of Scholasticism, Enlightenment, and Renaissance? Groups free of the absolutism of God and the feudal state could focus attention on the improvement of the conditions of the mind and body, pursuits labeled as sinful in an earlier age. The tale of Joan of Arc is perhaps the most vivid expression of the striving of an *entire class* of people for freedom from what, in the Middle Ages, might not even have been recognized as "oppression" (that which is viewed as "efficiency" in one age is often recognized as oppression in another). Feudal institutions could not possibly survive the empowerment of the group.

Philosophy/Theory/Event	Implication for Individuals	Implication for Organizations	Implication for the Fit Between Individuals and Organizations
Plato c. 428 - c. 348 B.C. Three capacities of man: reason, will, and desire. Men possessed by reason were to become the rational, ideal rulers of others. Men possessed of will were capable of being good soldiers, if led by reasoned men. Men possessed of desire learn to obey their rulers and can become good workers.	People can be segmented, by supposed abilities, into impenetrable, hierarchical, "classes."	Codifies organizational structure, where the leadership of "rational men" at the top curbs the more base instincts of those at the bottom.	As long as all parties agree to the underlying assumptions, workers will "accept their stations" in life.
St. Augustine 354-430 One of the most influential Christian figures, St. Augustine, extended the Platonic doctrine to include the distinction between the world of spirit and the world of flesh—a chasm still present in much current Christian thought.	Concern for "conditions of the flesh" (and of the mind) seen as sinful. Individuals accepted misery in this life in exchange for church-arbitrated life everlasting. Western World enters the Middle Ages.	**feudalism:** the system of political organization prevailing in Europe from the 9th to the 15th centuries having as its basis the relation of lord to vassal with all land held under fee and as chief characteristics homage, the service of tenants under arms and in court, wardship, and forfeiture. *Webster's New Collegiate Dictionary.*	The Church becomes the Platonic "rational man" to which others look for direction. The relationship between individuals and this organization (and to the feudal system) was one of dependency. Society ready to accept "pain" and misfortune in this world in exchange for "reward" in "the world to come."

TABLE 2.2a: A BRIEF HISTORY OF WORK

Philosophy/Theory/Event	Implication for Individuals	Implication for Organizations	Implication for the Fit Between Individuals and Organizations
The Magna Carta *1215* Demands for liberty signed by England's King John. Initially meant to apply to "any baron," the final edited version applied to "any freeman." This wording enabled the resurrected Magna Carta to serve as a model for 18th-century democratic revolutions.	Liberties enforced for members of the aristocracy.	Developing notions of liberty foreshadowed the downfall of feudalism.	Individuals would eventually begin to expect a wage in exchange for work and would, as feudalism collapsed, be free to move to where they could find opportunities for work.
St. Thomas Aquinas *1225-1274* Shattered Augustinian duality of soul and body making learning permissible both inside and outside of the Church.	Development of individualism. Individuals blessed with intellect (and a patron) were free to write great works, create great art, and invent machines like, for example, the printing press. Ushered in the ages of Scholasticism, the Renaissance, the Enlightenment, the Age of Reason in the 18th century.	Made possible the development of centers of learning and industry in cities.	The movement of people from the countryside to cities meant ready labor for the endeavors of industry and greater opportunity than had been found under feudalism.
Martin Luther *d. 1546* Extends Aquinas by asserting that the clergy had no mediating role between individuals and God.			

TABLE 2.2b: A BRIEF HISTORY OF WORK

Philosophy/Theory/Event	Implication for Individuals	Implication for Organizations	Implication for the Fit Between Individuals and Organizations
Thomas Hobbes *d. 1679* — Increase in individualism requires new justification for the rights of kings. Hobbes states that it is not through "divinity" that a monarch claims sovereignty, but rather, through a "social contract" between the sovereign and those willing to exchange individual liberty for peace and security.	By implication, individuals should be able to renegotiate contracts when they believe their leaders are not providing them with peace and security.	Reinforces the Platonic ideal of the rational leader with superior vision able to direct the efforts of others for the common good.	Hobbes may be seen as the point of initial divergence between rational leadership and acquiescent followership.
Adam Smith *d. 1790* — In *The Wealth of Nations*, Adam Smith makes the rational claim that the most effective form of organizing involves the division of labor into heterogenous tasks coordinated by those who manage the operation.		Organizations could become rational entities improved by the division of labor which made possible great gains in productivity.	Locke pulled toward a growing sense of "individuality" while organizations strived to reach the point where "…skilled labour gets progressively superseded, and will, eventually, be replaced by mere overlookers of machines" (Ure, 1835). The divergence between individuals and organizations had begun.
John Locke *d. 1704* — Claimed that no absolute statement or idea was exempt from the test of reason and empiricism. Also claimed that if the ruler overstepped the bounds of their "social contract" with the people, then the people were justified in overthrowing the leader.	Locke ushered in an age of revolution where whole societies came to believe in the preeminent importance of individual rights and liberties.		

TABLE 2.2c: A BRIEF HISTORY OF WORK

Philosophy/Theory/Event	Implication for Individuals	Implication for Organizations	Implication for the Fit Between Individuals and Organizations
Karen Horney 1885-1952 Horney suggested that our inborn "real self" is driven toward self-realization and potential. Given a sense of "safety" during life, this real self will flourish. Without it, we create an "idealized self" designed to protect us from a world trying to inhibit expression of "who we are." When the real self cannot be expressed, we display certain neurotic behaviors. We compulsively move toward people, complying with their every wish; we move against others, fighting against even the implication of control; or we move away from others, compulsively detaching ourselves from genuine relationships.	Horney's work shows how the imposition of systems and structures external to ourselves creates stress and neuroses.		Organizations require systems of order and rationality to achieve collective purpose, direction, and success. These systems, almost by definition, contradict the tendencies of the "real self" described by Horney. Many individuals in today's organizations understand this "compartmentalization" whereby they create safety by showing the "ideal self" at work and saving the "real" parts of their lives for evenings, weekends, holidays, vacations, and retirement. Compartmentalization merely defers stress.
Henri Fayol 1916 Henri Fayol's 1916 *General Principles of Management* outline characteristics of organizations: 1. division of work 2. authority 3. discipline 4. unity of command 5. unity of direction 6. subordination of individual interests to the general interest 7. remuneration 8. centralization 9. scalar chain of authority 10. order 11. equity 12. stability of tenure of personnel 13. initiative 14. esprit de corps	Fayol's model suggests conformity for success.	In spite of the tremendous variety of organizational changes this century, Fayol's fourteen principles continue to form the backbone of nearly every large organization.	

TABLE 2.2d: A BRIEF HISTORY OF WORK

Philosophy/Theory/Event	Implication for Individuals	Implication for Organizations	Implication for the Fit Between Individuals and Organizations
William James *d. 1910* James's *Principles of Psychology* extended empiricism to the concept of the Self; that is, no thoughts or emotions exist outside of the realm of "the knower". James argued that a person's constant stream of thoughts tended toward, or could tend toward, personal growth and the expansion of consciousness, saying, "Pessimism is essentially a religious disease."			
Frederick W. Taylor *d. 1915* Frederick Taylor's 1911 *The Principles of Scientific Management* captured the essence of the most revolutionary rationalist model of organization to date. Taylor claimed scientific management as a Darwinian idea in the field of management.	On a societal level, individuals (particularly in America) are to become far less likely to accept misery in exchange for salvation. Growing American wealth permits the individual development described by James.	Organizations able to presume a degree of rational certainty in labor cost and productivity. Scientific management schemes were the perfect adjunct to mass production workplaces. Tremendous profitability reinforces the use of rational models of management.	While Taylor intended his description of Scientific Management as a force for productive harmony and profit for employers and employees alike, the methods, in practice, tended to dehumanize employees. Where the goal of the division of labor was to simplify each and every task to such a degree that it could be performed by the "lowest form" of worker, scientific management drove employees to the breaking point in performance of their repetitive tasks. As James spoke of the human drive for growth and development, industry circumscribed both the motion and the free will of employees at work.

TABLE 2.2e: A BRIEF HISTORY OF WORK

The particularly American "Age of the Individual" had not yet been born. While John Locke wrote about the rights of the people to overthrow leaders who had violated their "social contract" with the people, it was John Stuart Mill who proclaimed that liberty was *the* fundamental pursuit of *individuals*. Freed, now, from the admonitions of the Greeks and the Church, any individual theoretically was free to find his own soil to till, his own knowledge and growth to pursue, his own profits to seek. New technologies made it possible for people to leave lands where their individuality was challenged or the opportunities less than desirable and sail to the New World to build their own dreams, saying "Don't Tread on Me" to central institutions attempting to coerce obedience. While the existence of slavery precludes any true assertion of the Age of the Individual, we must, again, remember that one age's "efficiency" is another age's oppression—any dilution of this recognition ignores the social, economic, and institutional forces that lead to injustices recognized only after transitional periods of liberation.

How did the modern organization form? Is it not miraculous that all forms of knowledge, technology, and society converged to allow the organizations producing today's marvels? No miracle, actually.

Evolution produced today's organizations, requiring an acquiescent pool of labor willing to participate over the centuries in the often deadly work of production. A society comprised of self-actualizing *individuals* would not have been able to build the pyramids, the Great Wall of China, or the ships that sailed from Europe to the New World in the fifteenth century. Organizing *requires* self-sacrificing participation and the Western world provided just such a labor force from the days of Plato to the nineteenth century when William James stated that "Pessimism is essentially a religious disease" and broke the yoke of a

reliably oppressable workforce.

Today's organizations exist because, given Western history, the formation of the modern organization was a *fait accompli*. They are because we are as we are.

Or, rather, as we were.

The paths of leaders and followers began to diverge in the seventeenth-century, with the redefinition of the Platonic ordering of leaders and workers by Hobbes who suggested that leaders ruled via a social contract with those being led, and by Locke who suggested that followers could remove leaders from power for violation of the social contract. No longer, as the

> **W**E SEE THE UNIVERSE
>
> THE WAY IT IS BECAUSE
>
> IF IT WERE DIFFERENT
>
> WE WOULD NOT BE
>
> HERE TO OBSERVE IT.
>
> —Stephen Hawking
>
> **ANTHROPIC PRINCIPLE**

French and American revolutions attest, were groups of people prepared to subject themselves to the rule of those they did not respect or trust. At the same time, the Age of Reason brought a "new rationality" to life as seen, for example, in the work of Adam Smith who explained how reason, rationality, and empiricism could be applied to organizations and, in fact, to entire economies. With powerful new tools presaging the age of mass production, newly empowered and newly individualistic rationalists and capitalists created institutions that persist to this day. While the owners and leaders of these new organizations were freed from Church strictures on learning, their workers by and large continued to accept their fates as young and old alike toiled in farms, factories, production houses, and workplaces of incredible tedium and torment.

The common path of the individual and the organization, a well-traversed trail of burgeoning prosperity nearly two thousand years long, was about to diverge. In the late nineteenth century, Frederick Winslow Taylor codified the best management practices under the rubric of *scientific management* and optimized the division of labor through the use of stopwatches, rules, and procedures. While he intended his methodology to be a force for the improvement of both the individual and the organization, in practice, the techniques pushed entire workforces to the brink of exhaustion in pursuit of efficiency and profitability. Meanwhile, William James taught that the restrictions of the assembly line were barriers to the most fundamental human drives toward self-realization, improvement, and growth. Later, psychoanalyst Karen Horney explained how people become neurotic in social environments that limit honest expression of the *real self* by demanding conformity to workplace cultural norms of the type characterized by Henri Fayol in *General Principles of Management*. The difference between the teachings of Horney and the management principles of Fayol is fertile ground for the humorous perspective of *Dilbert*. This same ground, this gap between our *expectations* of expression and the reality of organizationally limited behavior, produces a thin, accepted layer of stress that workers try to treat with vacations, sick time, health insurance, or retirement.

> **T**HE COMMON PATH OF THE INDIVIDUAL AND THE ORGANIZATION, A WELL-TRAVERSED TRAIL OF BURGEONING PROSPERITY NEARLY TWO THOUSAND YEARS LONG, WAS ABOUT TO DIVERGE.
>
> **THE BIRTH OF RESISTANCE**

It's true that today's work world is immeasurably more humane than it was even one hundred years ago. Conditions are better, pay is better, benefits exist, and people have more opportunities to chart their own lives than ever before, following their own direction between jobs, careers, and localities. Still, the basic processes of organizing are little changed from the forms described by Fayol. While management trends such as empowerment, teams, participatory decision making, quality, and the "learning organization," promise a place of self-development at work where the "real self" can shine, most realize that the true situation is often far closer to Fayol's than to Horney's—and Dilbert entertains in the breach.

THE BASELINE LEVEL OF STRESS

A baseline level of stress is present in every organization where the expectations of the individual and the requirements of organizing move in parallel—the more individuals expect the chance for the real self to show up to work, the more organizations develop new tools and process to channel common effort via the minimization of variation. And the monoculture reigns supreme.

The difference between the expectations of individuals and organizations provides a necessary tension in the workplace; much as a small labor surplus in the economy offers a reserve for demands of peak production, so does the baseline level of stress provide a ready source of momentum for required spurts of organizational energy. Take, for example, the company that needs to reorient itself in its market environment. The strategic repositioning can be tied to a revaluation of the individuals required to change in order to marshal their support for the change. The slogan "Working Together for Success Together," for example, captures the possibility of improvement for both the organization and the individual. Imagine the difficulty of motivating a workforce of self-actualized, transcendent employees! "Our Success Adds Nothing to Your Lives That You Do Not Already Possess" or "Our Improved Market Valuation Causes You to Re-Assess Your Values of Non-Attachment."

While the baseline level of stress in today's organizations can be seen as functional—fertile ground, if you will, for motivating organizational improvement—it is also, like a well-fertilized lawn, good culture for the rapid development of unwanted varieties. Often, under such conditions, all it takes is a light sprinkling of change to sprout varieties of stress and resistance that flourish amidst the field of desired behaviors. Like lawns ready for weeds, monocultures are sensitive to invasion by unwanted stressors.

The functional balance between our need to work and the stress produced by work remains intact until a major change occurs in our place of employment. Then, often without warning, our measures of accommodation can become overloaded as we find ourselves overstressed. Workplace stress caused by major change is not likely to diminish; if current trends and projections are accurate, we can only expect an increase in the frequency, rate, and complexity of changes to come.

Changes in organizational goals, systems, processes, and procedures add to the baseline level of stress found in any organization and we must ask, "Why?" While it is certainly fashionable for the leaders of organizations to assert that people just don't like to change, the case is made in this book that people just don't like the way organizations *implement* change. The following chapter illustrates the reasons why programmatic methods of change often add expensive and unnecessary stress to organizations implementing improvement efforts.

3

Programmatic Methods of Organizational Change

This chapter is a call for alertness. It asks us to examine the degree to which even the most participatory models of organizational development and change lead to the formulation of change as a commodity that is sold to employees—people who, while at work, are not generally able to say "no" as freely as they are to sales pitches outside of work. A halfhearted "yes" to change can lead to stress and resistance that diminishes the effectiveness of the changes you hope to implement in your organization.

Organizations cannot succeed without the improvements brought about by change. Even successful organizations are forced to reinvent themselves periodically in response to changing market, competitive, economic, demographic, and regulatory challenges. Change, as we all know, does not come without a price; it is difficult to do, and even more difficult to do repeatedly when each change may add to the baseline level of stress found in every organization. Add to this difficulty the fact that the accepted models of change—developed over the past one hundred years of relative stability and learned by leaders and change agents alike—are proving themselves to be less than perfect adaptations to today's world of nearly continuous change.

In this chapter we examine the accepted models of change, trace their evolution, and begin to describe the ways in which these models generate resistance to change and add to the levels of stress in today's workplaces.

In my organization development practice, I have worked closely with countless executives, managers, and supervisors who struggle with the difficulties of leading change. The frustration expressed by one senior government manager is shared by many I meet. He said:

> Last year I was asked to implement a process change to improve our handling of case backlogs, which I did. Then, two months later, I was contacted by the IS department and was told that my department had to change the way we processed cases to be in alignment with a new software package they were about to install. When I told my employees, they got ticked off at me because they just changed, and now here I was telling them they had to change again! The worst thing about this is that I did such a good job selling them on the first change that I had to undo my own work to get them prepared for the second. Since then, I've been asked to get their buy-in on several other changes and they've become cynical of everything I ask them to do.

His frustration was more about selling than about change—about having to pitch the merits of one change today only to have to do it again tomorrow with a different change. Continuous change frustrates managers and leaders, who have earned their success because of their ability to direct, coordinate, and produce, and who never expected to have to spend so much time and effort persuading others to change. And, to compound the difficulties, there typically is not enough time to complete one change before another must be sold, bought into, and implemented.

What has happened to organizational change? Why does it cause such consternation, resistance, and stress?

If you have ever longed for a new way to implement

organizational changes—without the selling, without the stress, and without the resistance—then you intuitively understand the paradox involved in attempting to get employee buy-in to changes they cannot rightly refuse. If you find the paradox somewhat disconcerting, then this chapter will help you better understand how it came to be and will give you background information you can use to make needed changes more effectively and efficiently in the future.

THE COMMODIFICATION OF CHANGE

Imagine yourself sitting in the waiting area of a large automobile dealership. A major sales promotion is in full swing, and you take in the balloons, streamers, and free cookies as you wait for your car to be repaired.

As you sip your Maxwell House, the television you are watching goes blank, flickers, and flames back to life with the vivid image of a cowboy on a horse in the middle of the car lot of the very dealership where you sit. As the cowboy implores you to trade in your car for a newer model, you search the magazine rack for a current issue of *Time, Newsweek, Car & Driver, Better Homes & Gardens*—anything to divert your attention from the cacophony of the television. Finding nothing worthwhile to read, you get up to leave the waiting room, hoping that your car is ready and you will be able to escape back home. At the moment you reach the door, an eager salesperson approaches with hand extended: "Have you heard about today's special on Sport Utilities?" he asks. "I'm just here for service," you say as you maneuver past. The salesperson lurches forward: "You should consider purchasing a service contract!" Inching past, saying, "No thank you," you make your way across the breezeway into the service area.

Midway to the service area, you are accosted by a mime, a sidekick to Cowboy Joe (the dealer's marketing is nothing if not eclectic!). The mime pretends to be you, driving into the dealership in your ancient wreck of a car, first saddened by your miserable lot in life, then ecstatic at the sight of all the new cars in the lot. When the mime turns to look with joy upon the car lot, you escape behind the building, pull out your cell phone, and beg for a ride home.

In the midst of Big Ticket promotional events for major programmatic organizational changes, many people simply divert their attention, sneak around, hide, or leave. As leaders and agents of change, we become blinded by the core assumption that people *must* choose the changes we sponsor because they are, in a sense, captive prospects for what we have to sell. The truth is much closer to the scenario just described: people can *check out* of their commitment to your organization just as quickly as you would turn tail and run from the cheesy promotional events described above. Even if they do not leave, they may become cynical or apathetic about the change. In times of high unemployment, they're more likely to stay but become disillusioned. When unemployment is low, talented people will leave for other opportunities when faced with heavily hyped change not directly related to the enhancement of work *at their level* and *from their frame of reference.*

> **comm·od·i·ty** *n* **1 a:** CONVENIENCE, ADVANTAGE **b:** something useful or valuable **2 :** economic good: as **a :** a product of agriculture or mining **b :** an article of commerce esp. when delivered for shipment **3** *obs* : QUANTITY, LOT (Webster's New Collegiate Dictionary)
>
> **c o m m · o d · i · t y**

Change is no longer a process. It has become a thing, as well it must to be handled effectively by organizations operating under norms of rationality. A process cannot be heralded as easily as a commodity can; it's just not as easy to describe. Before programmatic change can be hawked, it must be defined—commodified, if you will. The leaders of organizations, and the consultants they hire, have time-tested processes at their disposal to help them convert problems or opportunities into plans—processes that follow the general form described by Guiltinan and Paul in their 1982 textbook, *Marketing Management*:

▼ Conduct a situation analysis
▼ Establish objectives
▼ Develop strategies and programs
▼ Provide coordination and control

While the field of marketing cannot lay claim to the genesis of this simple four-step process, we must keep in mind the fact that the key capability of market economies is marketing. Tools and techniques shown to be of value to the field of marketing will find their ways into other related fields such as the management of change. This transfer of capability is as natural a process in business as the body's use of hemoglobin to carry oxygen to cells. Marketing is the oxygen of organizational life.

In organizations, we market as easily as we draw breath. Once a change is given a memorable name and defined with a vision and action plan, today's successful leaders understand what they must do to package their visions for change and sell them to other leaders, executives, boards, stockholders, employees, and customers. Persuasive messages of change are often displayed for all to see on image-adorned whiteboards that cover walls, tables, chairs, people, or anything else capable of display. Requests for

resources, in particular, are frequently accompanied by tremendously persuasive showmanship. In preeminent marketing cultures, ideas are clearly marketed like commodities.

Leaders in most large organizations market their change programs by expanding Guiltinan and Paul's basic steps ever so slightly with the help of human resource "communication specialists" who use a classic marketing formula to help them:

▼ *Research the audience* to understand the needs, drives, wants, and communication styles of those who may be targeted for activities designed to lead to persuasion.

▼ *Segment the audience* into groups with similar characteristics so that strategies can be tailored.

▼ *Develop strategies* for reaching each target group.

▼ *Evaluate and modify* their activities to ensure that maximum impact has been made and that the desired number and configuration of targets have been persuaded; strategies are modified to ensure the best possible result.

At times, the strategy selected to reach each group targeted for change will be as simple as deciding when to hold a briefing, meeting, or town hall session to tell people about the change. In more complex and professionalized organizations, in particular, management's persuasive strategies will involve more local work. Quality teams, task forces, reengineering groups, and cross-functional organization design teams seem on the surface like nods toward grassroots leadership of the organization. But in most cases they are tolerated because leaders have been led to believe the axiom, "Participation in organizational change leads to commitment to organizational changes." This belief stems directly from the limited research done in the 1940's by Coch and French in the Harwood Manufacturing Company and summarized in their statement:

It is possible for management to modify or to remove completely group resistance to changes in methods of work and
the ensuing piece rates. This change can be accomplished by
the use of group meetings in which management effectively
communicates the need for change and stimulates group participation in planning the changes (Coch & French, 1948).

While subsequent research has revealed the equivocal-
ity of this statement, the reality of organizational life is that
such approaches to change work as long as those "partici-
pating" accept that they are, in fact, planning the infrastructure to support management's communicated "need
for change." When we examine Coch and French's statement closely we can recognize participation for what it
has become—a thinly veiled means to lower resistance to
change. The connection between marketing and commitment, a link that literally spawned the entire field of organization development, was first forged by the work of Kurt
Lewin, a mentor of Coch and French, who was asked by
the U.S. government in the early stages of World War II to
devise a program that could be used to persuade house-
wives to serve liver and brains for dinner in place of more
desirable forms of meat in short supply because of the war
effort. Lewin found that simply promoting the consumption of these less desirable foods through the use of patriotic appeals was far less effective than another approach—
participation. He discovered that women who participated
in discussions about what could be done to persuade others to change their eating habits were ten times more likely
to eat liver and brains than were women who were en-
treated with stirring patriotic lectures. Lewin showed that
traditional marketing was less effective than participation.
It should come as no surprise, then, to discover that John
French was a student of Lewin's at Harvard, that Lewin
headed research at the Harwood plant, and that Lester
Coch was Harwood's personnel manager. After Lewin's

death, French carried on Lewin's research at Harwood. French, the academic, and Coch, the manager, welded the link between participation (merely a creative form of marketing) and commitment that lasts to this day—and lasts in spite of the realities of organizational life.

The marketing and organizational commitment paradigms diverge when we consider that persuasive communication in the marketplace leads to *internal commitment* to purchase on the part of consumers who are free to make up their own minds without fear of consequences. On the other hand, persuasive, marketing-like communication within organizations will tend to produce *external commitment,* compliance, if you will, as long as organizations continue to be characterized by norms of command-and-control. In many ways, the very use of quasi-participatory techniques during major organizational change limits the development of the internal commitment required of the organization's members to alter their work routines. As leading management scholar Chris Argyris recently said,

> For top management, then, the essential thing to know is that there are limits to internal commitment. Employees do not understand—in fact, they usually resent—executives preaching internal commitment while continuing to demand external commitment from the rank and file. Indeed, a great source of discontent in organizations is that top-level managers continually risk their credibility by espousing empowerment too glibly (1998).

While the marketing approach to change may not seem at all strange to most leaders and organization development specialists, the frequent lack of connection between executive strategies and the day-to-day realities of life in the operations makes it clear that the best alternative to a completely successful change—a change where motivated, committed people enthusiastically implement the new way—is a change where employees at least *comply* with the directives and mandates of the change. Since we can expect that an increasingly dynamic, turbulent, business climate will require leaders to make changes ever more quickly—via marketing—then we can also expect entire workforces to become less committed and more compliant. There are tradeoffs. In automotive design, engineers often must choose between precise handling and a soft ride. It is the rare automobile, indeed, that is able to accomplish both. Organizations that change rapidly do not always change completely.

Another reason for the increasing reliance on compliance rather than commitment is the gradual movement away from people-oriented change paradigms to those focused more on tangible, rational, technical processes. While acceptance of the philosophies of organizational change will continue to swing between the poles of the human and the technical sides of change, we are likely to find ourselves in a prolonged period of movement away from focus on the inter- and intra-personal aspects of change.

During the industrial revolution, technology, not philosophy, provided the impetus for the development of large, profitable organizations. During this period of time, humanism took a supporting role to rational scientific management. When the technology of the assembly line became commonplace by the end of the first third of the twentieth century, more humanistic models of leadership, management, and change provided organizations with the marginal improvements they required as rationality played the supportive role. Now, in the midst of the computer revolution, technology once again provides the most noticeable source of improvement. And, as in the industrial revolution, rationality and control bond people to their machines.

MARKETING THE CHANGES WE MANUFACTURE

Countless management books lining the shelves at chain bookstores present a wide variety of methodologies for the transformation of organizations; this book is one of that group. Watching the ebb and flow of management concepts seems at times like viewing an evening of one-act plays; just when you get used to one cast of characters and story lines, the lights dim and another takes the stage...all night long. Even with the diversity of offerings, though, the principles of marketing and rational problem-solving run like barely conscious metaphors just under the surface of the scripts. Here are some examples:

The Changemaker as Salesperson...The changemaker must treat the organization, or the team, as a customer, to be listened to, understood, fitted, and served" (Robbins & Finley, 1996, p. 109).

From the Table of Contents of *Leading Change*, by John Kotter:
The Eight-Stage [change] Process: (1) establishing a sense of urgency; (2) creating the guiding vision; (3) developing a vision and strategy; (4) communicating the change vision; (5) empowering employees for broad-based action; (6) generating short-term wins; (7) consolidating gains and producing more change; (8) anchoring new approaches in the culture.

In *The 21st Century Organization*, Warren Bennis and Michael Mische describe their "Phase I" of conversion to the twenty first-century organization. Phase I, Visioning and Setting Goals:
  1.1 Creating a Vision and Goals
  1.2 Identifying Opportunities
  1.3 Forming and Educating the Reengineering Team(s)
  1.4 Communicating the Vision and Gaining Commitment
  1.5 Establishing an Infrastructure.

Noel Tichy and Mary Anne Devanna, in their 1986 book, *The Transformational Leader*, describe activities relating to "Creating a New Vision:"
  ▼ diagnosing the problem
  ▼ creating a mobilizing vision
  ▼ mobilizing commitment
  ▼ getting people signed on to the mission.

Chapter titles from Gouillart and Kelly's 1995 book, *Transforming the Organization*:

Chapter One: Achieving Mobilization
Chapter Two: Creating the Vision
Chapter Three: Building the Measurement System
Chapter Four: Constructing an Economic Model
Chapter Five: Configuring the Physical Infrastructure
Chapter Six: Redesigning the Work Architecture
Chapter Seven: Achieving Market Focus
Chapter Eight: Inventing New Businesses
Chapter Nine: Changing the Rules Through Information
                   Technology
Chapter Ten: Developing the Rewards System
Chapter Eleven: Building Individual Learning
Chapter Twelve: Developing the Organization

In *The Challenge of Organizational Change* (1992), respected authors Rosabeth Moss Kanter, Barry Stein, and Todd Jick describe the "Ten Commandments for Executing Change:"

1. Analyze the organization and its need for change
2. Create a shared vision and common direction
3. Separate from the past
4. Create a sense of urgency
5. Support a strong leader role
6. Line up political sponsorship
7. Craft an implementation plan
8. Develop enabling structures
9. Communicate, involve people, and be honest
10. Reinforce and institutionalize change.

Robert Davidow, in his chapter entitled "Structuring the Change Initiative," from *The Change Management Handbook* (1994), says, "The communication strategy is a mechanism to let various stakeholders know what is going to change, why, and what benefits they can expect to derive from the change."

The basic principles of marketing and rational problem-solving form the structure of nearly every change and change implementation methodology recommended by today's most popular business authors. Most change programs share at least some of the following characteristics:

▼ The environment (customer needs, financial and legal characteristics, competition, technology, etc.) is assessed. Most typically the analysis takes place at the executive level.

▼ The organizational mission is clarified.

▼ The current state of the organization in terms of people, technology, machinery, financials, etc. is assessed and summarized.

▼ The gap between the environment and the current state of the organization is clarified.

▼ A vision is produced that helps the organization focus on the general characteristics needed to close the gap and achieve success.

▼ Goals and objectives set targets for change.

▼ Implementation strategies are devised.

▼ Implementation strategies are operationalized with associated roles, responsibilities, and accountabilities.

Most models of change management share a family tree with the principles of marketing, with the common progenitor being the rational belief that *all problems can be reduced to their root causes and assigned actionable solutions* (a perspective that echoes from Plato, Hobbes, Locke, Taylor, and Fayol). All too often, however, the search for tangible root causes blinds the problem solvers to the frequently intangible human dynamics underlying error, accident, and inefficiency. In one organization, for example, I was asked to help a work group that had been tracking error rates to identify the *tangible* root cause of their failings. The tracking increased their collective workload by nearly fifteen percent simply because no one was able to address the fact that serious conflicts between the group and its supervisor were diminishing the group's motivation to perform. Under the advice of a friend, the supervisor used time during a team meeting to ask if anyone could identify any group issues. Hearing none (no one was willing to call his behavior a "group issue"), he came to believe the conflicts were strictly between himself and a few unhappy team members and asked all team members to discuss their personal concerns with him alone during one-on-one meetings. With the main issue off the table, the search was underway for concrete problems and solutions. The group never resolved its difficulties because the leader treated subjective interpersonal issues as background. He

> **A** BUTTON IS CLICKED IN THE MINDS OF LEADERS AND CHANGE AGENTS, AND THE STANDARD TAPES OF HOW TO IMPLEMENT CHANGE BEGIN TO WHIR.
>
> **THE CLICK/WHIR RESPONSE**

believed that the more rational search for root causes would help his team. It was as if the seeker of solutions saw only the pointing finger.

Are today's change leaders mistaken in their gut-level use of these rational problem solving and marketing assumptions as they contemplate and implement change? Not at all. In many situations, this approach to change is perfectly appropriate. Genuine choice, however, does not always prompt managerial decision making. The use of problem solving and marketing tools is, for many, an automated response to the perceived need for change. A button is clicked in the minds of leaders and change agents, and the standard tapes of how to implement change begin to whir. Problems are addressed with solutions that are then marketed to the rest of the organization. When leaders use a "click/whir" response to a felt need for change, there is a chance that the automated response will be in less than perfect alignment with the precise path needed to ensure the most efficient organizational change. When alignment is off, as with the alignment of the wheels on a car, wear occurs. Wear, as we are about to discover in the following chapter, occurs in a variety of unexpected forms in our organizations.

The click/whir response of leaders to challenges and needed changes is rooted deep within the soil of bureaucracy deposited by the flood of industrialization pouring out of the Victorian era, and supported by thinkers as diverse as Socrates:

> ...over whatever a man may preside, he will, if he knows what he needs, and is able to provide it, to be a good president, whether he has the direction of a chorus, a family, a city, or an army.

...and Luther Gulick:

> It is clear from long experience in human affairs that...a structure of authority requires not many men at work in many places at selected times, but also a single directing executive authority. The problem of organization thus becomes the problem of building up between the executive at the center and the subdivisions of work on the periphery of an effective network of communication and control (1937).

Leaders often see themselves as the hunters of problems using the bow of rational problem solving and the arrow of marketing designed to hit targeted operations with change dead on center. Unfortunately, it's a moving target.

Conclusion

Accepted principles and practices of management and leadership attract the rationalist's marketing plan like lovers who have never been apart and never lost their passion. Lost in their mutual dreams of perfection, they are mesmerized by one another and cannot dream of being apart. And why should they? This tight bonding has enabled the creation of spectacular products, technologies, cities, and civilizations. Who are we to complain?

We are, in fact, very different individuals from those who came of age when these basic assumptions and structures were defined. While a scholar may find important similarities between the stopwatch of Frederick Taylor and the statistics of W. Edwards Deming, the reality is that people in today's workplace are much savvier consumers of leadership direction than were their great- and great-great-grandfathers. While the lovers of marketing and control spawned the organizations of today, people have developed along wholly separate lines. Organizations created carefully differentiated, specialized jobs to be directed by a professional management class, but World War II brought women and veterans to the workplace who expected their "piece of the dream" and joined unions when they felt that the balance of power swayed against them. While the development of information technologies allowed for the precise monitoring of performance, employees in the Sixties and Seventies, more diverse and aware than ever, began to use these same technologies to expand the scope of their learning about the "inner workings" of business. Where the teams and data tracking of the Eighties allowed for the improvement of quality, people learning to understand the fundamentals of their organizations also learned that their knowledge, in the face of organizational power and politics, was not always enough to make needed changes.

Where a computer on every desk now permits unforeseen levels of productivity, the operators of these same computers know how to log on to any number of Internet job search engines to help them move on when they feel as though their ability to make independent decisions on the job is being impeded by the same infrastructure of command and control that made possible the genealogy of their independence.

And yet, the parents, the happy couple of rational command and marketing, continue to believe the children will be swayed by the same inducements. It is as if the parent of an independent young adult still expects to persuade with promises of "an extra hour of television" and punishments of "no dessert after dinner."

The mesmerized models of change, blinded by the very real successes of the past, fail to notice their own habituated patterns. While the *content* of one change may differ dramatically from another, the *processes* of change—the ways in which changes are marketed to organizations—show precious little variety.

Most organizations continue to make changes by generating a plan (a program, if you will) for change, giving the program a memorable name, and promoting the program to employees. In the following chapter, we examine the ways in which a simple act—the naming of a change program—causes reactions to change expressed during nearly every organizational change effort.

Resistance to
Programmatic Change

In this chapter, marketing-like programmatic change is viewed as a source of resistance. This source is examined with the goal of helping leaders and change agents make informed choices about the processes they use to change their organizations.

The changes implemented during this century have revolutionized our world. They also have caused great pain and upheaval. While we can not always expect change to be easy or welcomed, we can expect that the same level of creativity and innovation found in the improvements brought by change should also be identifiable in the processes of change. As we demonstrated in the previous chapter, most processes of organizational change share the basic assumptions of marketing and problem-solving. As such, they lead inexorably to the creation of marketing-like change programs that are driven from the top of the organization. While change typically should start with the top of the organization, it isn't the source of change that causes resistance that slows the change—it is the process by which change is sold to the rest of the organization.

SOURCES OF RESISTANCE TO CHANGE

I once worked with a young professional whose remaining parent lay dying in a nursing home not far from work. This young woman was the reason the father came to town to die—he knew he would be cared for. The woman's supervisor did not grasp the impact of the pressures she faced in her personal life and continued to assign her a full load of important projects.

> *"Why,"* I asked her, *"have you not leveled with your boss and told him about the pressure you're facing?"*

> *"I don't want to disappoint him,"* was her reply.

This talented woman chose not to disappoint her boss when her father had barely a month left to live. She made the conscious decision to devote much of her intellectual and emotional energy to her boss even as she, a woman of considerable compassion and sensitivity, devoted equal emotional energy to her father. In essence, she chose to please *two* authority figures in her life: her father and her boss.

This poignant situation illustrates the power leaders hold in the lives of people at work. A leader might be boss, confidant, taskmaster, authoritarian, disciplinarian, and may even supplant the roles of actual parents. Like parents, leaders often have the authority to give names to those underneath them.

THE POWER OF NAMING

Groups—community groups, family groups, groups of friends, work groups, work teams, units, departments, and divisions—have identity.

The name of a group, department, or division (e.g., "Human Resources," "Merchandise," or "Region Five") is a definitive property that conveys identifying information about that group's character and activity. Often the explicit name is less relevant than the behaviors, beliefs, and underlying assumptions found in a particular group:

▼ We take care of one another here.
▼ We are family.
▼ We are efficient, profitable, and humane.
▼ We trounce the competition!
▼ We are a team.
▼ Whatever it takes!
▼ We like to take it easy around here.

While not "names," per se, these principles of behavior and culture act as names inasmuch as they convey important information about the group in question. Centrally driven programmatic changes that run counter to these deeply held identifiers of group character will tend to be seen as threats by members of the group to which they are applied. To the extent that the change requires the group to fundamentally alter who they are, through the acquisition of new skills, technologies, or processes, group members may come to fear loss of identity. While many a well-intentioned leader believes they are not asking the targets of change to change "who they are" during a change program, we must remember the degree to which our roles are imbedded deeply in our identity. When, as leaders, we make clear our expectations that individuals, groups, units, and departments must change, we are, in effect, asking them to change *who they are*. Irrespective of the perceived merits of the change, people in a changing organization

will often fear loss of identity—the loss of name. They may openly resist, or more dangerously to the ultimate success of the change, they may simply feign compliance as a way to minimize the risk of identity loss. Others may change readily, recognizing an opportunity for improvement and renewal.

The Mighty Beast and the Un-Named Man

The great beast lumbers through the room. It grabs hold of human *hors d'oeuvres* and devours them. "This is carnage!" someone screams. We weigh our options. We consider fleeing. We abandon thoughts of resisting the overpowering force, yet joining this juggernaut would only diminish our sense of self. We decide, instead, to outsmart the beast by pretending compliance, encouragement, and participation. Secretly, we hope the beast becomes so drunk with power that we will seem insignificant and will be freed to make our way home.

> THE MASTER'S RIGHT OF GIVING NAMES GOES SO FAR THAT IT IS PERMISSIBLE TO LOOK UPON LANGUAGE ITSELF AS THE EXPRESSION OF THE POWER OF THE MASTERS
>
> —Frederich Nietzsche
>
> **THE POWER OF NAMING**

The preceding paragraph might have conjured visions of "organizational paradigm changes," "Project X," or "reengineering" in your mind's eye. Or, perhaps you recognized the parallel between the paragraph and the tale of Odysseus and the Cyclops in Homer's *Odyssey*.

Odysseus, far from his home at Ithaca, happens across a vicious, man-eating Cyclops. Desperate to survive this threat and to stem the loss of men to the appetite of the Cyclops, Odysseus planned, then later executed, his response:

"Cyclops, here, have a drink after that jolly meal of mansmutton! I should like to show you what drink we had on board our ship. I brought it as a drink-offering for you, in the hope that you might have pity and help me on my way home..." He took it and swallowed it down. The good stuff delighted him terribly, and he asked for another drink:

"'Oh, please give me more, and tell me your name this very minute! I will give you a stranger's gift which will make you happy!'"

...Then I gave him a second draught. Three drinks I gave him; three times the fool drank. At last, when the wine had got into his head, I said to him in the gentlest of tones:

"Cyclops, do you ask me my name? Well, I will tell you, and you shall give me the stranger's due, as you promised. Noman is my name. Noman is what mother and father call me and all my friends."

Then the cruel monster said, "Noman shall be last eaten of his company, and all the others shall be eaten before him! That shall be your stranger's gift."

As he said this, down he slipt and rolled on his back. His thick neck drooped sideways, and all-conquering sleep laid hold on him; wine dribbled out of his gullet with lumps of human flesh, as he belched in his drunken slumbers (Rouse, 1937).

Upon the giant Cyclops' collapse into drunken stupor, Odysseus and his men drove a large sharpened pole deep into the single eye of the monster, thereby blinding it and permitting their escape. When the Cyclops screamed in agony for help, his likewise cruel and oversized comrades asked him what had happened.

"Noman put my eye out!" was his anguished reply. "Well," they replied, "If no man is using force, and you are alone, there's no help for a bit of sickness when heaven sends it so you had better send your prayers to Lord Poseidon, your father!"

The tunnel-vision-suffering Cyclopsean Executive Committee essentially emasculated their colleague for his having fallen to an invisible, unnamed, foe.

And what of Odysseus?

> With these words away they went, and my heart laughed within
> me, to think how a mere nobody had taken them all in with
> my [craftiness]! (Rouse, 1937).

How many of us, in the face of a heavily promoted programmatic change, feel as Odysseus' men did as they watched others being devoured? With fear as the lens of perception we wear during times of change, we hope to intoxicate our leadership with the visible artifacts of our undying support and respect. We dutifully attend meetings and produce the documents of compliance even as we secretly hope the much-hyped program will lose direction (sight) and leave us unscathed. When threatened too deeply, either through reasoned response to a massive transition, or as a result of innate personality characteristics, we may overtly or covertly attempt to "blind" the organization through subversion, counter-advocacy, or even sabotage. Ironically, Odysseus' plan succeeded through covert means. By losing his name, he was able to outwit the Cyclops and gain his freedom. What are we so afraid of when organizational change is afoot?

FORMING AN ATTACHMENT TO WORK

Perhaps we become attached to the expectations we develop about our lives at work. Daryl Connor (1993) said that the root of negative reaction to change is the loss of control we fear when change threatens our personal *status quo*. The expectations we hold about ourselves, our jobs, and our identities give us a sense of predictability and order—control, if you will—in our lives. In my work, for example, I typically can expect to arrive at work, catch up on my e-mail and telephone messages, review my calendar, and begin my day of meetings, workshops, group sessions, and data analysis, guided, for the most part, by the needs of my clients. This quasi-predictability helps me order my life and make sense out of daily events both at work and at home.

When our attachments are threatened, we can become fearful. Peter Marris (1986) explained that our attachment to our expected work roles and situations is a necessary prerequisite for getting work done. Early researchers on the topic of infant bonding to caregivers (Harlow, 1958; Bowlby, 1969) demonstrated how this drive for attachments begins in infancy and affects the development of the individual. Bowlby (1960, 1973) described the typical reactions of infants who were separated from their parents. The stages of *initial protest, despair,* and *detachment* sound eerily similar both to the stages of grieving and loss outlined by Dr. Elizabeth Kubler-Ross in her 1969 book *On Death and Dying,* and the stages of response to changes described by William Bridges in *Transitions* (1980).

This basic feeling of bonding individuals often have for organizations is not unbreakable. People at work, like young adult children, do tend to "fly out of the nest." But do the reasons for turnover have anything to do with people's desires to "spread their wings?" Research seems to indicate that turnover is more a function of severed attachments than a desire to find a better opportunity elsewhere. In a 1991 review of research on the relationship between employee commitment to organizations and employee turnover, Meyer and Allen found three types of commitment that influence employee decisions to stay or leave. These types are: (1) affective commitment (the employee's sense of emotional attachment to the organization); (2) obligatory commitment (the employee's sense of obligation to the organization); and (3) continuance commitment (the employee's evaluation of the difficulties and costs they would face were they to leave the organization. Although Meyer and Allen suggested that these three types of commitment would correlate negatively with an employee's decision to stay or leave, subsequent research by Whitener and Walz (1993) and Jaros (1995) found the strongest negative correlation between affective commitment and intent to quit. We take this evidence to suggest that people are likely to stay with their organizations when they feel a sense of emotional attachment to the organization and are likely to leave when this attachment is severed. This research suggests that the work of Bowlby, cited above, may be more relevant to turnover than previously thought. Like the young who form attachments to caregivers, we cling to our organizational roles with an often profound attachment which, when broken, can motivate us to sever our ties and leave.

We value the expectations we develop about our working lives—about the form, function, and actions that take us through our days—and we are often knocked off-center when these expectations are threatened. We do not, however, tend to "go silently into the dark night of change." Rather, in many cases and in many ways, we rage against the changes we are told to make at work. What form does our resistance to change take? While the following chapter documents the way resistance detracts from the return-on-investment (ROI) of change, it is worth taking a moment here to explore a few of the defense mechanisms (Freud, 1936) that are activated when our expectations about work are threatened:

▼ We *repress* unpleasant feelings we may have about the change, and about past changes we have experienced. A person who is repressing personal reaction to change is merely postponing the inevitable response.

▼ We *regress* and take on activities or opinions that have protected us in the past. Take, for example, the supervisor who was promoted for his technical skills in spite of his significant deficit in people skills. When a change is announced, this supervisor may not be able to provide the interpersonal support and leadership needed by people who believe that their expectations are being threatened. Unable to draw upon these capabilities during this stressful time, this supervisor might regress to the technical and problem-solving skills that served him well in the past. This supervisor might direct his employees into a narrow problem focus which, while comforting, might prevent them from gaining a richer understanding of the "big picture" of the change. People who are in regression can develop a tunnel vision that leads them to over-focus on particular areas of their work and neglect others.

▼ We *project* our own less-preferred and less-accepted personal characteristics onto others. If, for example, I have a drive for power that can be seen by others but not by myself, then I may ascribe motivations of power to those calling for a change. I might believe that leadership is only "out to get what they can for themselves," all the while missing the very real benefits of the change to myself.

▼ We engage in *reaction formation* by going overboard, displaying feelings and behaviors diametrically opposed to the ones genuinely felt. If, for example, I am filled with rage at the prospect of reporting to a new boss, I may exaggerate the opposite feeling by letting everyone at work see nothing other than my support for the change. I may send flowers to the new leader or make promises to that leader I will not be able to keep.

▼ We go into *denial* about the personal impact of the change. We say things like, "It's all a bunch of hot air. My job will be the same next year as it is today. This will blow over." While changes may blow over, denial, as a defense mechanism, can prevent us from learning the very skills and behaviors we need in order to benefit from the change.

Defense mechanisms provide some comfort to the ego in the face of changes that threaten to break our attachments. At the same time, they may slow our adoption of even the most beneficial changes.

Cognitive Resistance to Change

The fundamental cognitive calculus undertaken when we are confronted with change is this:

> *Will I respond to this change by seeing it as a fit with my preexisting expectations and opinions, or will I adapt my expectations and opinions in order to accommodate the change?*

Our expectations about the relationships and tasks we find at work allow us to generate scripts about what works for us and what does not. These scripts, or "schemas" contain information about the culture of our workplace, the nature of our relationship to authority, the demands of our tasks, and the scope of control we have over our performance. According to Wofford (1994), scripts or schemas are the data we hold internally about the "objects, events, roles, conditions, sentiments, and outcomes that occur in a sequential pattern in familiar tasks and situations" (p. 181).

Assimilation and Accommodation

Borrowing from cognitive developmental psychologist Jean Piaget, we can say that when an person's scripts match the demands and nature of her work and her workplace, then she is in a state of cognitive *equilibrium*. That is, her scripts are predictive of her daily reality—her expectations match her experience. When a change is perceived, as when one is told to report to another supervisor, *disequilibrium* occurs; our hypothetical employee's scripts or expectations may no longer match her experience. Typically, when in a state of disequilibrium, we are driven to restore the balance, the equilibrium, between our expectations and our experience. This we can do by *assimilating* our perceptions of the change into the scripts we already have about change or *accommodating* our scripts to the realities we perceive. If people have experienced poorly managed changes in the past, they may assimilate perceptions of the current change into the scripts they hold for past experience with change ("Here we go again!" "We're going to have to document everything." "Another flavor-of-the-month."). If people have experienced well-managed change, their assimilations will likely be more positive. Assimilation can be viewed as an inherently *conservative* cognitive mechanism inasmuch as it seeks to preserve the scripts already possessed rather than to create new scripts, new options, or new expectations. Preservation of current scripts maintains equilibrium in the face of a potentially unbalancing reality. People with negative perceptions of past changes will likely be very resistant to change if they assimilate new changes into old schema. People with positive perceptions of previous changes will be likely to adapt fairly quickly to the new change as long as the assumptions of the new change are consistent with those of earlier changes.

Our hypothetical target of change can also restore equilibrium by allowing her scripts and expectations to be altered by the change. Required to report to a new supervisor, a person with this approach to the restoration of cognitive equilibrium will tend to allow the change to formulate *new* scripts about work. "Well," she might say, "here's a chance to learn something new," or "I'll have a chance to build relationships with some influential people." While accommodations are not always so positive, the point to

remember is that the accommodating strategy is a potentially *innovating* one where new ideas, opinions, skills,
and relationships become possible.

Leaders also have choices when they discover resistance to the changes they make in their organizations. They
can assimilate the resistance into preexisting scripts about
the nature of employees. Many leaders assimilate resistance into a schema with these beliefs:

▼ Resistance is a normal part of the change process.

▼ People resist because they do not understand the
change.

▼ We can do a better job of educating and training
our employees so they can come to see the benefits of the
change.

▼ Understanding the benefits of the change will decrease resistance.

When encountering resistance, this schema can produce a self-reinforcing loop that exacerbates the problems
as leaders offer additional programmatic responses to
"solve" the problem of resistance.

An "accommodating" leader is not necessarily one who
is permissive. When perplexed by the response to change,
a leader who tends to use the cognitive strategy of accommodation to disequilibrium may see behaviors others would
term "resistant" as being unique to the situation being observed. S/he could adjust preconceived notions of how
people "should" respond by saying:

▼ "Wait a minute here! People in this organization have
always understood our goodwill in the past. Why wouldn't
they now? I'm not sure more training is the answer. Why
don't we sit down with a focus group of   people and
learn what's up with them?"

▼ "Maybe they're acting this way because they have a
better idea of how we should make this change."

Accommodation is essentially an innovative strategy in

that it leaves room for new outcomes not addressed by preexisting schema, scripts, and expectations.

While some readers may be tempted to review this section in the hope of finding nuggets they can use to develop a training program to help a workforce learn to accommodate change, caution is advised—that's probably an assimilation strategy!

Motivation

Motivation is the linchpin issue in organizational change. While everyone may need to use a new database system, for example, the speed and thoroughness of conversion to the new system will depend to a large degree upon the motivation of people asked to make the change. Poorly motivated, they may drag their feet, fail to completely learn, or, in some cases, feign proficiency with the new system in order to appear compliant and motivated. On the contrary, people who recognize the direct value of a change to the immediate tasks they have to perform at on the job are more likely to be sufficiently motivated to change. The case of the USAirways transition from a proprietary reservations system to SABRE, the industry standard, is characteristic of the result of insufficient employee motivation for change. USAirways management sold the SABRE reservation system as a required change for both Y2K compliance and for improved reservations flexibility into the future. One merely had to travel by air during the first few months of the transition to understand just how frustrated and demotivated USAirways gate employees were during the transition. Many said the new system was more complex, less intuitive, and far less customer-friendly than the one it replaced. Long lines and employee willingness to vent characterized the change. Discussion with various employees indicated that some of their colleagues were simply "taking some time off" during the change.

Motivation can inspire us to work beyond our own expectations and accomplish surprising feats of ingenuity, production, and excellence. Maslow (1943a, 1943b) and Herzberg (1966) suggested that we are motivated in varying degrees by the everyday needs for safety and security and by the more esoteric needs for psychological growth and self-actualization. While Maslow claimed that each need was motivating to the degree that lower-level needs had been met, Herzberg suggested that basic needs such as a fair wage and predictable benefits are not inherently motivating. He looked to the "higher order" needs for achievement, recognition, and control as needs that motivate us to perform at our best. Herzberg's ideas suggest that finding a way to help people meet higher order needs in the course of a change would motivate them to participate in the change. We see this in organizations when people get turned on by the possibility of learning new skills and accepting new challenges during a change. Most leaders and change agents operationalize Herzberg's ideas by either: (1) making pitches to their employees about the benefits of the change (the marketing approach); or (2) by acting as if participation alone will be seen as a self-actualizing opportunity by employees. Unfortunately, as we learned in the previous chapter, marketing works best in the absence of the types of authority relationships found within organizations. Regarding the motivational value of encouraging people to participate in the design, development, and implementation of change programs, experience shows that it is often only a select group of people who participate, leaving the rest to be motivated by other means, typically in the implementation stages of the change. Hackman and Oldham (1976) offer a model that explains why some people are motivated by joining in the planning and implementation of change programs while others are not. Their model first considers the concept of the meaningfulness of a particular task. Consider, for example, participation in the planning and/or implementation of change. According to Hackman and Oldham, people find their jobs meaningful based upon the fit between their personal preferences for the types and numbers of skills they use on the job (skill variety), their need to see their contribution reflected in the total work (task identity), and the degree to which their work "matters" to people inside or outside of the organization (task significance). A person who, for example, prefers to use a limited set of skills on the job (low skill variety), does not need to know how their work moves a project forward (low task identity), and does not particularly need to see how their work makes a difference (low task significance) would probably be demotivated by the opportunity to sit on a committee that had to use a wide variety of individual and team skills (high skill variety) and individual effort to move a project forward (high task identity) so that the organization could be meaningfully changed to improve performance and worker satisfaction (high task significance). In fact, the autonomy of the change team and the rich feedback environment typically found therein would likely frighten off our hypothetical employee. Lest we think it is our job as leaders and change agents to increase the skills, commitment to the whole, and sense of importance of all, we might wish to consider that doing so may be inherently de-motivating to people whose preferences are simply different from ours.

We argue that motivation for participation in change programs is best found in those areas where day-to-day, real-time, win/lose issues are addressed by the change itself. Motivation has been oversold and used as a justification for countless training programs and change strategies that miss the point—people change when their lives are made more rewarding *from their perspectives* by the changes they consider making. A case in point:

An employee in a large financial institution is asked to come to a meeting where the topic of "self-directed work teams" (SDWTs) will be presented by the divisional executive and the senior human resource representative for his area. All who attend the meeting are told about the benefits of SDWTs and persuaded that they will learn new skills, have a better understanding of the whole company and how their efforts contribute to the company's excellent products. They are told that on a SDWT they will be better able to see how their individual and team work matters to internal and external customers. At the end of the meeting, the employee takes an extended break with his five closest friends and colleagues where they discuss their apprehension about the change.

Contrast that example with this:

People in a competing financial institution are asked to come to a meeting where a divisional executive will introduce a special new team who will work with their division. The role of this team is presented simply as this: "They are to learn what you need to do your jobs better and to help you get what you need." Our person in question recognizes several members of the special team as former colleagues who were good performers and good friends to people in the division. The executive adds, "Let's not beat around the bush here, folks. As many times as I try to walk your areas with my leadership, there's no way I can understand your work like you do. You are the experts and we on the executive committee would do well to listen, learn, and use this special team to help you get what you need to do your jobs better. Now, I know what you may be thinking. You might think 'Well, if you really want to make our lives easier, send us new computers and ten more employees!' I appreciate your frustration. I also expect that you will respect the boundaries within which we're operating here. One of the roles of this special team is to learn about the really unique things you're doing in this division that make you so successful at what you do. Then, we're expecting this team to come to us and teach us the winning ideas so we can support them in this division and, where appropriate, offer them to other areas in the company. And, where you haven't figured out how to solve a problem or do something better, we're expecting this team to consult to your needs to help you find your answer."

At the end of the meeting, our person approaches two of the special team members, catches up on some personal stories, and makes a lunch appointment for the following week.

Which scenario would you prefer to see in your organization? Which has more total potential motivation? Which has created less total resistance? Which is most likely to lead to positive change?

Perception

By definition, any change program is likely to stand out from the background of organizational life. An organization with a track record of poorly or incompletely implemented change will likely feel the temptation to more heavily and completely support and market subsequent change programs, thereby "raising the bar" of visibility for

WE NOTICE WHAT STANDS OUT FROM THE BACKGROUND

change programs. Unfortunately, as we have discussed, the more heavily promoted a change, the greater the likelihood of resistance. For these reasons, mere visibility guarantees nothing in terms of the motivating potential of a particular change program—a marketing mistake. The perspective of people who perceive the change significantly determines their reaction to the change. A "Big Event" launch for a program or change merely activates perception; it does little, if anything, on its own to determine the motivation of those who attend.

Characteristics of the Perceiver

Author Wayne Dyer once said, in a clever play on words, "I'll see it when I believe it." In organizations, scarce resources, the presence of fear, and competition leave many believing they are threatened. Although many are motivated to perceive potential opportunities, these ambitious individuals are often perceived as threatening by others.

According to Kathleen Ryan and Daniel Oestreich, authors of *Driving Fear out of the Workplace*, five factors operate to create a "pattern of threat" in an organization:

▼ Actual experiences in the present or in a past situation—what has happened directly to the person and what has been directly observed;

▼ Stories about others' experiences, especially those who are liked or trusted;

▼ Negative assumptions about others' behavior and intentions, based on private interpretations about what has happened;

▼ Negative, culturally based stereotypes about those with different levels of organizational power;

▼ Externally imposed change.

Apart from the obvious relevancy of the last of these factors to the topic of this book, it takes little imagination to understand how threat and fear surface in organizations during times of change. Employees whose perceptions are characterized by fear may be well-motivated to see the fearful aspects of a change. Fear, when present, alters perception. When a change program, because of its novelty, stands out against the background hum of everyday worklife, employees who feel fear tend to perceive the change from within this context. In such a state, people will reach for whatever they believe will minimize their fear. Unfortunately, the defense mechanisms they frequently engage at such moments can produce stress and resistance, leaving them less accepting of the change.

Organizations, often characterized by authority relationships and fear, create a significant base of employees who perceive change negatively. It is paradoxical but frequently true in experience: the more novel the change—the more it stands out against the background hum of organizational life—the more likely it will produce resistance. The greater the degree of resistance accompanying a change, the greater the expenditures required to see the change through to complete acceptance and implementation.

Attribution

A fundamental basic assumption of organizational change is *participation begets participation*. This assumption is axiomatic in the organization development profession. After all, why develop participatory models of organizational change if we do not assume that one employee's support of a change will result in the eventual support of others? Another relevant question is, "What thoughts or feelings would a person have about other people who actively support the change?" This question has power, especially because change is such a visibly social phenomenon.

A basic tenet of attribution theory is this: When someone changes behavior because of what we determine to be external causes [such as compliance with a change], we

cannot be certain about the sincerity of their actions (Organ and Batemen, 1991).

Put another way, when we see people enthusiastically change behavior in response to a well-sponsored initiative, we tend to ask ourselves, "Are they doing this because they have to or are being rewarded for doing so?" When we believe others are complying with a change because they have to or because they receive some form of reward for doing so, then we tend to place their sincerity in doubt. When we doubt those who advocate change, then the likelihood that we will overtly or covertly resist the change increases. The greater the resistance, the more "payment" or "pain" we will demand to comply with the change. The accumulation of payment or pain is a significant contributor to the overall cost of change programs.

Additionally, if the change or the people who promote it falter in some way, the fundamental attribution error ("When other people mess up, it is because of their personal flaws, but when I'm at the center of a problem or failure, it is because I was a victim of circumstances") confirms, in our minds, the lack of credibility of those in charge. Throughout the organization, these thoughts can take root:

> When a change runs into snags, it is obviously because leaders are incompetent and the change is unrealistic and wasteful. Of course, when we have difficulty mastering the new computer system or reporting to the new supervisor, it is most certainly not due to our characteristics and behaviors. Obviously, the blame rests with the misguided change forced upon us from those out-of-touch, incompetent, glass-ensconced suits!

Attribution works to disconfirm the sincerity of those who support the change if we believe those supporters are better off in some way for proclaiming their support. And, when changes run into snags, as all do at some time or other, we look to those in charge as the cause of the failures. On the other hand, when we have difficulty implementing aspects of the change, our first thoughts are not usually with our own shortcomings.

LIBERTY AS A BARRIER TO CHANGE

The following statement by John Stuart Mill outlines a fundamental, even unconscious, assumption of most U.S. workers. This idea of individual freedom is a source of resistance to change in many organizations:

> Human nature is not a machine to be built after a model, and set to do exactly the work prescribed for it, but a tree, which requires to grow and develop itself on all sides, according to the tendency of the inward forces which make it a living thing (*On Liberty*, p. 123).

Even if we disagree on scientific or cultural terms with the totality of Mill's statement, we cannot deny his gift for accurately defining Western notions of the meaning of liberty. As members of a relatively egalitarian society, Americans do not tend to like to have their lives altered by someone else. We also tend to respond less than favorably to the "renaming" of our workgroups.

▼ We are no longer a Quality Circle. Now we are the "Productivity Team."

▼ They've stopped calling us a task force and started calling us a "suggestion group."

▼ We've been able to take it easy on this team for so long and now they're asking us to participate in this Work Process Change program.

Requiring change of a work group's identity places group members in a psychological state similar to that of a woman faced with the cultural imperative to change her last name to her husband's on their wedding day. According to Anne Bernays, co-author of *The Language of Names*,

DONT TREAD ON ME

"Whenever a woman marries, sheds her name, and substitutes her husband's, she's also shedding part of herself, part of who she's been since birth. Whether she's conscious of it or not, if she changes her name her marriage will be lopsided, like a scale with five pounds of nuts on one side and two on the other." Major changes threaten core elements of the identities we carry in our lives at work, at home, and as members of a society that cherishes liberty.

Conclusion

Giving a change program a widely proclaimed name is the first major expense incurred during the change process. Unfortunately, during the period of initial hype, these back-end-loaded expenses aren't even on the radar screen. If they are discussed, they are dismissed as "acceptable losses" that happen with any change.

We propose that by refusing to promote catchy names for change programs implemented in today's organizations, we proactively "outwit" resistance to change. If not, we, like the Cyclops, may find that "mere nobodies" can derail expensive changes.

As we will see in the following chapter, organizational changes that alter expectations and sever emotional attachments increase the factors that increase costs to the organization. Organizations that appropriately adopt new models for change will gain competitive advantage by being able to change more quickly, more completely, and more efficiently than competitors using programmatic change methods.

5

The Bottom-Line
Costs of Resistance

*In this chapter, we examine the fallout from or-
ganizational change by looking at various types
of organizational dysfunction found during
change. We also indicate the financial cost of such
dysfunction—costs that diminishes the return on
investments made to improve organizations.*

In the novel *Under the Net* by Iris Murdoch (1954), the
character Hugo Belfounder was said to have endeavored to live a life free of generalizations; walking amongst
the flowers, he supposedly refused to see the generalized
pattern of "a garden," opting instead for the careful examination of each unique blossom.

> What I speak of is the real decision as we experience it; and
> where the movement away from theory and generality is the
> movement towards truth. All theorizing is flight. We must be
> ruled by the situation itself and this is unutterably particular.
> Indeed it is something to which we can never get close enough,
> however hard we may try as it were to crawl under the net
> (80-81).

What Change is Like on The Line

Bob, a front-line supervisor, and his staff of twelve welders work in the manufacturing division of a large, national heavy equipment company facing challenges from overseas competitors. Bob and his group have just attended a corporate presentation on the new project called "Working Smarter." In the presentation, held at a large concert hall in the center of the city, senior executives and external consultants told of the millions of dollars being invested in automation projects and described the self-directed work teams that were about to be formed in each division. A videotaped presentation by the CEO, complete with rousing images and stirring music, announced the Working Smarter slogan and promised better financial and stockholder performance as a result. Each of the 1500 divisional employees in attendance left the event with a Working Smarter baseball cap, mug, pen, and business-card-sized refrigerator magnet imprinted with the new corporate values for the change. Bob and the dozens of other supervisors present also left with the knowledge that they would soon be required to become "members" of the self-directed teams—as equal partners rather than as supervisors. The message to the supervisors was clear: those who could not handle the transition would find it difficult to find a role in the company.

On the way back to the shop, members of Bob's group rename the corporate program "Working Madder," such is their anger about the process automations and their beliefs that the changes will threaten their jobs. Francis, a welder for seven years with the company, says, "I'll be damned if I'm going to have to fight for my job by learning how to run a computer welding system! I didn't get into this work because I wanted to push buttons for a living. I can make a hell of a lot more money on my own without all this headache!"

That afternoon, a group of employees, many of whom feel as strongly as Francis, go to Bob's office to ask for his opinion of the change. "We trust you." Jim, a senior employee, says, "You'll tell us the truth, just like you always do. Should we be worried about this?"

"Just keep your head down," Bob replies.

Four months later, as the first automated welding system arrives for installation, Bob will find his area decimated by absenteeism, time off, and illness. Bob, himself, will be known for frequenting the local pub and will tell his wife that he is genuinely unable to cope with the transition to the new system and to his new role as a team member. Ultimately, the system will be installed. The new team—with all of the original members still on the job and with Bob as an "equal" member—will seem to have made the change. It will take one full year, however, for the team to complete certification on the new system—three times the industry standard for similar conversions, but just about average for other teams in the company.

What happened? Why will Bob's team do so poorly in the transition to the new system?

While organizational theorists and change leaders may debate the merits of the self-directed work team approach and the way in which it was implemented in this case, we assert that the causes of resistance preceded, not followed, the implementation of the changes. Resistance begins when people find something to resist. "Big Ticket" events—those kickoffs characterized by large gatherings, senior executive participation (live or via videotaped presentations), and a plethora of slogans and values—provide ready kernels for the formation of resistance. While countless communication consultants extol the virtues of the Big Event, research is clear about the superior persuasive efficacy of face-to-face communication (Smith, 1982). Unfortunately, the span of control in many organizations makes face-to-face communication with each employee an expensive proposition. So leaders take the advice of consultants who suggest that the changes be introduced at large events with catchy slogans, giveaways, and executive presence. Unfortunately, these boisterous events feed the mistrust of senior leadership often felt by workers and produce the types of cynicism found on Bob's team.

THEORIES, METHODS, AND HOW-TO RECIPES FOR THE PROMOTION AND IMPLEMENTATION OF LARGE-SCALE ORGANIZATIONAL CHANGE ABOUND AND SPRING FORTH WITH EQUAL FANFARE FROM THE SAME SOURCE AS DO THEORIES OF MARKETING, ADVERTISING, MASS MEDIA, AND POLITICAL CAMPAIGNING.

THE SOURCE OF PROGRAMS

For Bob's team, resistance initiated by the Big Event was compounded by the to-be-expected response to the self-directed work teams approach. Without the initial resistance, leaders might have been able to implement the people and technical process changes without creating a level of resistance leading to absenteeism and dysfunction. In this case, the total load of resistance and stress would become so severe it would impede the team's ability to assimilate the changes and satisfactorily learn the new systems and processes. Like a miserable first impression, the cynical response to the Big Event hardens employees to the merits of proposed changes and produces a downwardly spiraling cycle of negativity and stress that slows the progress of change and jeopardizes the health of the organization's workforce. Then, illnesses, accidents, substance abuse, and grievances become the too-frequent companions of change.

Theories, methods, and how-to recipes for the promotion and implementation of large-scale organizational change abound and spring forth with equal fanfare from the same source as do theories of marketing, advertising, mass media, and political campaigning. Senior leaders not explicitly schooled or trained in these models of change learn them implicitly as consumers in today's demand-driven economy. These models are so deeply ingrained in the professional psyche that it is difficult to see them as anything other than "Truth." Like residents of resort towns who only visit local sites when guests come to town, many of us do not recognize our own milieu because we are too close—and too busy. The Belfounder character urges us to "see what we see" instead of seeing only the patterns of reluctance and persuasion balancing about the fulcrum of change. When we critically examine the accepted models of change, we discover the unintended outcomes created each time change is treated as a commodity—as a thing to be marketed to captive consumer-employees.

We begin by outlining the image of stress in the workplace, follow with a discussion of change-related stress, and conclude in sharp focus on the costs of resistance and stress to today's organizations. The thesis of this book is laid bare here: *programmatic organizational change adds unnecessary stress to your workforce—stress that subtracts from your profitability and competitiveness.*

THE PACE OF CHANGE

Nearly a half century ago, an episode of *I Love Lucy* offered a poignant allegory for the way we tend to react to the increasing pace of change found in today's workplaces. In "Job Switching," Lucy and Ethel, believing they needed to do something more lucrative than "homemaking," took jobs at a candy factory. The set for the factory floor was simple—a hole in the wall dispensed candies on a conveyor belt for Lucy and Ethel to wrap. Unfortunately, a broken switch on the conveyor caused it to accelerate out of control. Lucy and Ethel were a bit confused at first, not understanding what was happening. Soon, they became anxious and irritable as they frantically tried to adapt to the increasing speed of the belt. As the pace outstripped their ability to keep up, candies began to back up and fall unwrapped to the floor. They endeavored to work more quickly, to wrap intermittently, to eat the candies they couldn't wrap, even to fill their shirts with unwrapped candies in the vain hope that their failure would not be discovered. Ultimately, the pace became too extreme and they fell away, exhausted and helpless.

Changes flow through today's workplaces like the candies on that accelerating conveyor belt. When the conveyor of organizational change proceeds at a fast clip, with one change supplanted by ever-more complex changes, people begin to lose their ability to keep pace. Changes brought on by globalization and dispersed information access will increase pressure on organizations to keep up—to make legitimate changes to compete more successfully, or to make symbolic changes to offer the appearance of adaptation for the benefit of customers, shareholders, or regulatory bodies. Increasing the rate of adaptive or proactive change can be seen as a positive strategic development for an organization if it enhances the organization's fit with its market or service environment. At the same time, however, the increasing rate of needed or symbolic change adds to the baseline level of stress found in organizations and increases the likelihood that individual workers, and, in many cases, entire workforces, will become dysfunctional.

Future Shock

In 1970 Alvin Toffler published *Future Shock*, a prophetic book that carefully described the challenges faced by humans living in a world of ever-accelerating change. To Toffler, humans are "unprepared visitors" to the culture of dramatic change found in today's world. It is as if we, recent residents of the forest, have been transported forward in the blink of an evolutionary eye into a culture of fast music, fast machines, fast information, and accelerating rates of complexity and change. Movement has occurred too quickly. This period of human history characterized by mass production, industrialization, computerized information flow, huge cities, and nuclear families instead of clans is but a single nucleotide on a strand of DNA on a gene for "resilience" on the chromosome of a being whose total genetic makeup differs from that of a chimpanzee by only 1.6 percent. In short, we humans are ill-prepared for the pace and complexity of change in today's world. When our ability to assimilate change is outstripped by the pace of change we face, we are prone to the dysfunctional reaction Toffler suggested with the title of his book—*future shock.*

Toffler described three general stages of the future shock reaction. First, we become confused or disoriented, distorting our reality to control our concern. We feel lost in our own office space. We rise with reluctance in the morning, finding it difficult to motivate ourselves to make the trip to work. When we arrive, we seek out our former colleagues at familiar coffee pots and pretend the change "isn't that bad, really." Or, we may hide in our cube hoping the change will pass us by. We may fear our organization and become reluctant to expend extra effort, for extra effort leads to visibility that increases the likelihood our underlying fear will be discovered. We may put in less time at work or show up late after breakfasts or long lunches with friends or co-workers who share our concerns.

Second, as the pace of change increases like Lucy and Ethel's assembly line, we may become tired or burnt out. We may opt to leave the organization to those better equipped to deal with the changes. We may have moments of pronounced anxiety at work, fearing for our positions, or periods of inactivity as we find ourselves unable to get anything done. We leave early. Or, we don't come in for a day or two. Or three. Worse yet, we may attempt to work through

> **P**ROGRAMMATIC ORGANIZATIONAL CHANGE ADDS UNNECESSARY STRESS TO YOUR WORKFORCE, STRESS THAT SUBTRACTS FROM YOUR PROFITABILITY AND COMPETITIVENESS.
>
> **THE PROBLEM WITH PROGRAMS**

these periods of confusion, increasing our rates of error, mistakes, or accidents. We may grow irritated at the organization, at our colleagues, at our supervisors, at ourselves. We may express our anger privately through substance abuse or outwardly through violence in the home or workplace, all because we are unable to cope with the continually increasing onslaught of changes being made at work.

Third, we may retire. Many of us take early retirement, others retire on the job, entering prolonged periods of burnout during which we add little value to the organization, to our families and friends, to ourselves. In this stage of reactivity, we siphon resources from organizations needing our hearts and minds, not just our bodies, and we add immeasurable expense to those forced to move us aside to make needed changes. We may grow depressed or develop a serious illness, all because we suffer from the symptoms of future shock.

THE STRESS STUDY

In a classic study of human response to change and stress, Thomas Holmes and Richard Rahe (1960) surveyed thousands of people from several cultures about their perceptions of the most stressful events in life. Each person was asked to rank, from most stressful to least stressful, these life events. Surprisingly, there was strong agreement across cultures about the sources of stress. From this data, Holmes and Rahe were able to assign numerical rankings to stressful life events, as shown in Table 5.1.

Holmes and Rahe then administered their ranked instrument to another large group of individuals whose medical histories they were able to research. Their findings were astounding: anyone who earned a "score" of 200 or more points in a single year had a 50-50 chance of developing a serious (though not necessarily life-threatening) illness within the following year. Individuals with scores of 300 or more increased this significant health risk to 75 or 80 percent for the following year.

The work of Holmes and Rahe shows that high levels of stress are positively correlated with the incidence of health problems. How much of this stress is caused by organizational life? And, of this proportion, how much is due to organizational change, in general, and to programmatic organizational change, in particular?

A quick (non-scientific) review of the Holmes and Rahe scale indicates that first-order organizational factors (those items directly related to organizational factors such as "Business readjustment," and "Fired from work") account for 6 percent of the total in the scale. Extrapolating from the scale, we could say that 6 percent of stress-related illnesses occur as a result of stress in the workplace. Of course, the cause of workplace-related stress cannot be limited to first-order causes. What if, for example, a "Major personal injury or illness," occurred at work? What if a "Change in

Life Event	Scale Value
Death of a spouse	100
Divorce	73
Marital separation	65
Jail term	63
Death of a close family member	63
Major personal injury or illness	53
Marriage	50
Fired from work	47
Marital reconciliation	45
Retirement	45
Major change in health of family member	44
Pregnancy	40
Sex difficulties	39
Gain of a new family member	39
Business readjustment	39
Change in financial state	38
Death of a close friend	37
Change to a different line of work	36
Change in number of arguments with spouse	35
Mortgage over $10,000 [1971 dollars]	31
Foreclosure of mortgage or loan	30
Change in responsibilities at work	29
Son or daughter leaving home	29

TABLE 5.1: THE HOLMES AND RAYE STUDY

number of arguments with spouse," with 35 points, developed over one's mate's difficulties on *their* job? These second-order factors (factors caused by workplace stressors) add significantly to the overall rank score total, pushing work-related factors to nearly 20 percent of the total score values. Using this logic, we could estimate that of all people with scores of 300 or more, roughly 20 percent of their stressors would be related to work. We might even be conservative in our estimate. The St. Paul Fire and Marine Insurance Company says in their 1992 "American Workers

Trouble with in-laws	29
Outstanding personal achievement	28
Wife begins or stops work	26
Begin or end school	26
Change in living conditions	25
Revision of personal habits	24
Trouble with boss	23
Change in work hours or conditions	20
Change in residence	20
Change in schools	20
Change in recreation	20
Change in church activities	19
Change in social activities	18
Mortgage or loan less than $10,000 [1971 dollars]	17
Change in sleeping habits	16
Change in number of family get-togethers	15
Change in eating habits	15
Vacation	13
Christmas	12
Minor violations of the law	11

SOURCE: L. O. Ruch and T. H. Holmes (1971). Scaling of life changes: Comparison of direct and indirect methods. *Journal of Psychosomatic Research, 15* (1971), 224.

Under Pressure" technical report (cited by the National Institute of Occupational Safety and Health in its 1999 publication, *Stress*), "Problems at work are more strongly associated with health complaints than are any other life stressor—more so than even financial problems or family problems." Goetzel et al. (1998) claim that health care expenditures for workers who report high levels of stress are nearly 50 percent greater than for those who report lower levels of stress. With 40 percent of workers reporting that their jobs are "very or extremely stressful" (Northwestern National Life), we begin to wonder if it is true that 40 percent of workers have health care expenditures that are 50 percent greater than others simply because of the amount of stress they experience in their jobs on a daily basis. These percentages suggest that approximately 25 percent of employee health care expenses could be due to the high levels of stress at work. This should come as no surprise to the many readers who have experienced this correlation in themselves or in their organization. According to the American Institute of Stress, a New York City-based nonprofit organization founded in 1978, 75–90 percent of visits to primary care physicians are for stress-related problems. With large companies paying an average of $4,037 in health benefits per employee (William M. Mercer, Inc.), the case could be made that elimination of unnecessarily high levels of stress could save a company more than $1,000 per year in health care costs *per employee*!

While baseline levels of stress produced by the activities of production are absorbed within the cost structures of most organizations, societal and marketplace realities demand an ever-increasing pace of change. While increases in the pace of change can be expected to increase the likelihood of future shock in an organization, failure to change the way change is implemented will compound this dysfunction.

THE COSTS OF ORGANIZATIONAL CHANGE

In this section, we document the cost of the stress produced by organizational life and organizational change. While the contribution of programmatic organizational change to these costs is not known at this time, the reader who has spent time "on the line" knows full well how quickly the pomp of a newly announced, centrally driven change program can be converted into the cynicism and stress that drains an organization's resources—a process of reversed alchemy.

The following costs associated with organizational change are examined in this section: (1) inefficient change; (2) workers' compensation; (3) turnover; (4) absenteeism; and (5) substance abuse.

Inefficient Change

When is change efficient or successful? Your answer to this question depends upon your role in a change process. As a change sponsor, your answer might be: "This change will be successful when our goals are achieved," or, "This will be an efficient change if it happens on schedule." As a change agent, you might say: "The change will be successful when my services are no longer required." As a person experiencing change, you might find yourself saying: "This will be a successful change if it makes our work more productive," or "…if I get to keep my job."

Because of the variety of perspectives involved in the assessment of any organizational change, it is notoriously difficult to pin down data indicating the success of programmatic organizational changes. Nevertheless, studies of a variety of specific types of programmatic organizational changes do indicate less than desirable results. Studies of downsizing, for example, indicate that fewer than 50 percent of companies that downsized achieved their desired outcome targets (*Fortune*, 1994; *American Psychological Association Monitor*, 1994; Gilmore, 1994; McKinley, Sanchez & Schick, 1995). Other studies indicate similar results for Total Quality Management (*The Economist*, April 18, 1992, pp. 67–68; Arthur D. Little survey, 1992; Ernst & Young, 1992) and reengineering initiatives (CSC Index, 1994).

On the other hand, executives, consultants, and change agents alike tout the benefits of the changes made in their, or their client's, organizations—often citing significant returns on investments made in change. So, who is right? Do large-scale organizational changes add value or are they exercises in drama designed to impress employees, stockholders, and regulatory bodies?

The answer to this question is the holy grail of organization development research. It is notoriously difficult to accurately determine the return on investment (ROI) of organizational change. For this reason, change often feels like soothsaying, with proponents of one methodology or another proclaiming the bottom-line contribution of their approach. Why is accurate assessment so difficult?

To paraphrase Nunnally (1978), we can be confident in assessments of the ROI of a change program if the following is true: (1) we can clearly identify the behaviors, activities, and events that constitute "the change program;" and (2) there is no doubt at all about the relationship between the change program and the production of desired behaviors, processes, activities, skills, etc. in the "changed" organization. The first assumption presumes that we can understand and identify the specific aspects of a change that lead to change. The second assumption presumes there actually *is* a relationship between change programs and organizational improvements. If these assumptions are met, we can believe, with some degree of confidence, that one particular change program or another would lead to a particular return on investment. We could, then, call a particular approach to change either "efficient" or "inefficient" depending upon the relationship between the expense of the program and the tangible benefits produced by the program.

Unfortunately, in human affairs, it is difficult to determine the precise configuration of events that constitute "a change." Was, for example, a team leader excited about a change because of the skills she had the opportunity to learn or because she knew that, by learning the skills, she would be more visible to management? Did a company's process improvements lead to productivity enhancements or did the company become more productive because, in the process, it laid off ten percent of its workforce, leaving the other ninety percent working harder?

We can be reasonably sure of one thing, however, as per the discussion of change and stress earlier in this chapter: change often leads to stress, and stress leads to outcomes, like illness, for example, that add cost to an organization's bottom line. A more costly change is, therefore, a less efficient change.

Change, and the way it requires people to alter what they do, who they are, and the perceptions they have about their security, produces resistance that can slow a change. A somewhat typical example of this point occurred in a university that implemented a major information systems conversion. Although the "Big Event" promotional style is not generally used in universities to introduce non-academic organizational changes, internal communications quickly buzzed with official positivity about the well-named initiative. The faculty, already a rather cynical lot, were taken aback by the scope of the changes. They objected to the millions of budgeted dollars being charged academic units to pay for the change and cited the expense as evidence of the administration's willingness to play free and loose with resources they believed would be better applied more directly to educational and scholarly activities. Faculty pressured the deans, who exerted pressure on the administration to reverse course. Cries of academic freedom were also heard from the university's autonomous and powerful colleges who complained that greater homogeneity of administrative and academic functions would drag the strongest of the university's colleges, schools, and academic programs down to the level of the weakest.

These conflicts slowed the change, forcing standing teams to remain together much longer than planned, thereby siphoning resources from the departments donating team personnel. The time horizon for the change continued to extend beyond all expectations, and political control of the implementation of the change was passed around like the proverbial hot potato. In the midst of the upheaval, several unions threatened to strike should their worst fears be brought to fruition by improved systems requiring fewer employees thereby triggering future layoffs.

All involved knew that at some point the change would be made—the new systems would be installed, users would be trained, and students ultimately would benefit from the improvements—yet the cost of the change increased beyond anyone's expectations merely because the naming, marketing-like promotion, and top-down method of implementation produced initial resistance, stress, and dysfunction that were difficult to overcome. This centrally driven change program with its catchy name and aggressive communication strategy had became a screen upon which people projected their fears. No change so burdened with negativity can become as successful as initially hoped. Cost and time overruns drain efficiency from big-ticket programmatic changes and diminish their overall effectiveness.

There is one main way which any change can become less efficient than the full potential brought by the good ideas and needed improvements it contains. Even the most meaningful change, when named and hyped throughout the organization, is dragged down by the resistance and stress produced by reliance upon the marketing paradigm of change.

An article entitled "Change" in the April, 1997 edition of the magazine *Fast Company* offers a rare exposition on the inefficiencies produced by programmatic organizational change:

> If you come in and announce, "Here's the next change program," you're dead, says US West's Bob Knowling, a seasoned change agent. "You've just painted a target on your chest."

...and:

> In fact, even if you are the CEO, and theoretically in a position to compel people to perform, when it comes to change, you're liable to create your own worst nightmare: people quit, but stay; people say "yes," but do "no"; people go through the motions, but don't perform.

Workers' Compensation

Consider these typical problems in your workplace:

▼ Accident rates increase in areas of your organization meeting the accountabilities set forth in a new performance review system.

▼ Safety awareness seems to be lost during a reorganization.

▼ People seem to suffer more and more from non-specific "over-exertion" and "soft tissue" injuries after a department cuts back on available overtime hours.

▼ You find people making "mental distress" claims against your company after a reshuffling of management.

A common contributing source to these indices of dysfunction can be found in the dynamic human response to programmatic organizational change. A common "bucket" for the costs of these undesirable outcomes is your company's workers' compensation insurance pool.

Workers' compensation was the first widely utilized social insurance program in the United States, beginning in 1908 and gradually expanding to cover all states by 1949. Because workers' compensation is administered by individual states (various statutes and programs cover federal employees and those who work in a few select industries), a great deal of variance occurs by state in all aspects of the program. Workers' compensation covers the cost of work-related accidents, injuries, and illnesses and, for the most part, indemnifies employers against legal actions for such covered incidents. A worker who has an accident at work, or suffers from a work-related illness, is eligible for assistance under workers' compensation, which pays both medical fees and a significant proportion of lost-time wages. Employers purchase workers' compensation insurance from the insurance industry, or, in some cases, from the state. Employer participation in workers' compensation is mandatory in all but three states. Where mandatory, employers can choose to opt out of participation if they can demonstrate their ability to cover claims through self-insurance. Workers' compensation insurance premiums are not inexpensive and are based on the nature of work performed by a company and on the number and costliness of accidents that tend to occur there. Organizations and industries with a large number of work-related accidents and injuries pay dearly for workers' compensation insurance: In 1992 alone, the estimated total amount of workers' compensation premiums paid by U.S. organizations was approximately $70 billion, up 15 percent from 1989, the first year for which figures were available. It is estimated that premium costs had increased at a steady 15 percent per year until 1998 when, according to the *1998 RIMS Benchmark Survey* by the Risk and Insurance Management Society, Inc. and Ernst and Young LLP, the net cost increase slowed to 3 percent. The cost of workers' compensation premiums to individual employers is staggering—for every $100 of payroll, each employer pays between $1.50 and $15 in premiums, depending upon a variety of factors mentioned above.

A total of 6.1 million accidents and illnesses were reported in private industry

> IN 1995 THE AVERAGE COST PER WORKERS' COMPENSATION CASE WAS $4, 832.
>
> **THE POTENTIAL LOSS**

workplaces during 1997, resulting in a rate of *7.1 cases per 100 equivalent full-time workers* (Source: United States Department of Labor, Bureau of Labor Statistics, *News*, 12/17/98). In 1995, the average cost per workers' compensation case was $4,832 (Source: National Council of Compensation Insurance, Inc. 1996).

Underwriters and accountants lament the fact that the workers' compensation system is particularly easy to scam. A 1996 study by Conning Insurance Research and Publications (Hartford, CT) showed that more than 33 percent of the total amount of fraud absorbed by the property/casualty insurance industry (the category under which workers' compensation is classified) was due to fraudulent workers' compensation claims, thus making it the largest single source of fraud in the insurance industry. Because the workers' compensation system is run by individual states, there is no mechanism in place to trace fraud or those who commit it. In addition, any review of transcripts from workers' compensation boards and state and federal court records reveals the worker-friendly bias of many of these bodies.

Legitimate or otherwise, the physical accidents and injuries covered by workers' compensation represent tremendous expense to any organization. But, are they the only type of covered injury?

Change and Mental Distress

Physical accidents, illnesses, and injuries are not the only occurrences covered by workers' compensation insurance. The system is increasingly paying claims for mental distress. In a 1988 study, the National Institute for Occupational Health and Safety examined the leading types of work-related disease and injury in the United States. Psychological disorders made the top ten. Many states now recognize stress-related emotional or mental disorders as compensable under workers' compensation. The increase in payments for emotional or psychological claims had become so steep in California, for example, that in 1992 they were the leading occupational disease claim type. Although more recent workers' compensation reforms in California have brought these rates down, an increasing number of state and federal courts are expressing a willingness to uphold compensation board decisions in favor of employees claiming emotional distress as a result of workplace conditions (Walter & Sleeper, 1997; *Occupational Safety & Health Reporter*, 1998). Although recent decisions make the point that stress resulting from "normal" working conditions is not compensable, the following case, which resulted in a compensatory award of $800,000 and punitive damages of $2.25 million against the plaintiff's employer, illustrates how even a simple change program designed to bring new ideas to a management team can lead to disastrous results:

> ...in a Texas case, a 60-year-old paper company vice president was reassigned as an entry level supervisor in a warehouse. The vice president had more than 30 years' experience in the paper business and a college degree but was placed under the supervision of an individual in his 20s. This demotion occurred during a corporate transition to a young managerial team. The former vice president was subjected to age-related verbal abuse and was ultimately reduced to sweeping the floors and cleaning up the employee's cafeteria (Walter & Sleeper, 1997).

As this story documents, a company in the midst of an executive-sponsored programmatic change can go to extreme lengths to ensure compliance with the change especially when, for good reason, it is reluctant or unable to simply terminate employees or managers for non-compliance. Things can get out of hand quickly and result in rather expensive damages. It should be noted that in this case the plaintiff's compensation for work-related emotional distress vastly exceeded his award for his age discrimination suit.

The work of practitioners and researchers alike indicates the degree to which the very conditions found during the implementation of programmatic organizational change can likely be correlated with factors that lead to accidents and injuries covered by workers' compensation programs:

Job Conditions That May Lead to Stress (*National Institute of Occupational Safety and Health*):
- ▼ The design of tasks
- ▼ Management style
- ▼ Interpersonal relationships
- ▼ Work roles
- ▼ Career concerns
- ▼ Environmental conditions

Five key factors increase risk [for the generation of compensable claims] during reengineering (Witherell and Kolak, 1996):
- ▼ Fear enters the organization
- ▼ Employees can become confused and frustrated
- ▼ Morale declines
- ▼ Employees become overwhelmed by workloads
- ▼ Accountability for safety can be lost

From Peak (1997):
Organizations undergoing downsizing see increases in stress-related disability claims.

Goldberger and Breznits' *Handbook of Stress: Theoretical and Clinical Aspects* lists the following correlates of stress considered in occupational stress research, all of which can be salient during organizational change, particularly during programmatic organizational change:

▼   Deadlines
▼   Time pressures
▼   Machine pacing
▼   Organizational or administrative irrationality, red tape
▼   Workload, overload
▼   Responsibility load
▼   Participation
▼   Availability of intrinsic rewards
▼   Availability of extrinsic rewards
▼   Poor labor-management relations
▼   Loss of job
▼   Demotion
▼   Qualitative changes in job
▼   Overpromotion
▼   Transfer of job locus
▼   Change in shift pattern
▼   Role ambiguity
▼   Role conflict
▼   Role strain
▼   Degree of control over work processes
▼   Feedback and communication problems
▼   Job complexity
▼   Relationship to supervisor
▼   Ambiguity about future, job insecurity
▼   Quantity-quality conflict

A study, in 1993, by the National Institute for Occupational Safety and Health (NIOSH) documented how workers suffering from repetitive motion injuries reported stress of the following types:

▼   High work pressure
▼   Lack of decision-making authority
▼   Job insecurity

While the total amount of workers' compensation costs attributable to programmatic organizational change is not currently known, the experience of those close to change in today's organizations would suggest that the amount can grow to frightening levels. The cost for stress alone is staggering. Max Douglas of Indiana State University cites a United Nations International Labor Organization report that says job stress costs American business an average of $73,000 *per employee,* for a national total of $200 billion. Even a small percentage of this total amount tied empirically to programmatic organizational change represents a tremendous loss to America's corporations—to your corporation.

While research needs to be done to examine the precise correlation between the implementation of programmatic organizational change and the production of unnecessary change-related stress, the links do appear to be present. The message seems clear: reduction in programmatic organizational change will reduce future shock, which will in turn reduce the stress felt by people at work. A reduction in this unnecessary stress may ultimately save companies literally millions of dollars in workers' compensation payments.

Turnover

One morning, as I scanned through the radio stations in Orlando, Florida, I listened to a caller to a popular FM talk-format radio station:

> **Caller:** Yeah, I was listening to your station this morning and my boss came into my office all pissed off. She says to me "I don't ever want to walk out of my office and hear that garbage again! Turn that radio station off now!"

> **Host:** So what did you do?

> **Caller:** I told her that I'll listen to whatever I want to listen to and I quit right then and there. Hey, the Sunday paper is *full* of jobs. I'll take the weekend off, watch the girls on the beach, and find a better job Monday morning!

Host: What do you do?

Caller: I'm a warehouse manager.

Table 5.2, below, indicates that the caller probably is right about being able to find another job.

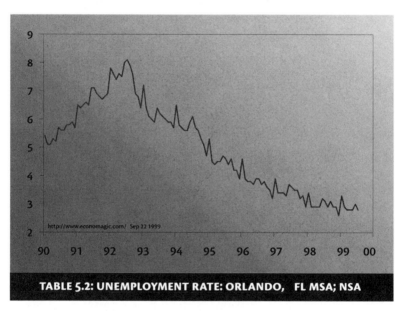

TABLE 5.2: UNEMPLOYMENT RATE: ORLANDO, FL MSA; NSA

In fewer than five years, the unemployment rate in Orlando fell *by nearly two-thirds*. The warehouse manager, presumably possessing a significant degree of training and expertise, probably will have no trouble finding another job after his weekend of fun at the beach.

You might conclude that the departure of the warehouse manager may actually have yielded a net positive to his company, given his apparent personality. In fact, a substantial body of research suggests that employee turnover can provide desirable outcomes to organizations through the exodus of low-performing (and frequently higher-paid) employees (Baysinger & Mobley, 1983; Osterman, 1987b). At the same time, the real world experience of turnover in organizations in today's tight labor market is unequivocal: it hurts. With unemployment in 1999 at or below 3 percent in many parts of the United States, the cost of search, selection, and training of new hires fills human resource and management ranks with dread. People whose organizations provide them with a degree of predictability (relatively stable expectations) are likely to be attached to, and more likely to stay with, their employers. People require a degree of trust in leadership in order to perceive proposed changes in a manner that leaves room for motivated participation. When employers announce major changes, many people instinctively question the stability of the expectations they hold about the organization. They ask, "Will I still have a job?" "Can I keep up with the new technology?" and "Will I have to alter my work/life balance?" The more major the change, the deeper the questioning and the greater the fear. Waves of pomp and presentation rock the boat of organizational performance and fill it with the water of resistance and fear. The more water, the more people bail. We can expect that organizations rocked by programmatic change will experience greater turnover than those making change in quieter ways. If your firm sits in a tight labor market, you can gain competitive advantage by planning and implementing changes in ways that maximize positive perception and motivation and minimize turnover. Let your competitors increase their costs with programmatic change. You can find a better way.

Absenteeism

"I can't deal with those process maps again tomorrow! I'm taking the day off!" "I've had it up to here with 'Customer Friendly!' I'm calling in sick!" You've heard these comments before, haven't you? You've likely even made some yourself. We know, intuitively, that employees are more likely to call in sick when they feel pressured and stressed by major change. The same employees who report record high levels of stress on the job are also failing to showing up for work in record numbers. According to the benchmark annual *Unscheduled Absence Survey* by CCH Incorporated, unscheduled absenteeism rates have risen 46 percent since 1994. The finance/banking industry, roiled by a continuing stream of mergers and downsizings, reported the greatest annual increase of 42 percent in the most recent survey (1998). CCH estimates that unscheduled absenteeism costs each company an average of $757 per employee. Why are people calling in instead of coming in? The survey indicated that only 22 percent of those who called in to report their absence claimed illness as their reason for staying home. Although family issues are still the leading reason reported for missing work (26 percent), the fastest growing reason is stress, cited 16 percent of the time in 1998 but only 6 percent in 1995.

Other research has shown the link between occupational stress and absenteeism rates (Seamonds, 1985), and job satisfaction and absenteeism (Muchinsky and Tuttle, 1979) suggesting that stressed-out and dissatisfied employees are much more likely to be absent than people who are less stressed and dissatisfied.

If you are a senior leader or a change agent, walk into any workplace other than your own during the initial stage of a major programmatic organizational change. The telltale signs of stress will surround you as you listen to people's fears, concerns, and cynicism about "the next big change." Notice how leaders will tend to offer newsletters, meetings, and training programs to employees in an effort to better educate them about the merits of the change. Listen carefully to front-line managers and supervisors, as well, as they describe to you the difficulties they have keeping their work areas adequately staffed. When you return to your own organization, remember to take with you the vision that recognizes excessive absenteeism as a symptom of changes treated as commodities and marketed throughout the organization.

Substance Abuse

Stress in the workplace is positively correlated with substance abuse by workers. Margolis, Kroes, and Quinn (1974) showed this to be true for "escapist drinking." Conway, Ward, Vickers, and Rahe (1981) found similar results for smoking and the over-consumption of coffee. Watts and Short (1990) discovered that stressed-out teachers were more likely to use amphetamines, alcohol, and marijuana than their nonstressed colleagues, while the healthcare industry has long explained that its relatively high rates of substance abuse on the job are due to the availability of medications and the special intensity of stress faced each day by those who work in medical facilities. None of this is to suggest that workplace stress leads to addiction, for, as Tim Sheehan, vice president for Minnesota Recovery Services at the Hazelden Foundation, says "Factors such as a stressful workplace or unhappy home environment don't make people alcoholics, but they can contribute to the relapse of someone working through recovery."

While stress at work might not lead to addiction, substance abuse does lead to employer expense: (1) substance abusers are three to four times more likely to be injured at work than non-abusers; (2) 47 percent of all accidents, and 40 percent of all fatal accidents, at work are caused by people who abuse substances; (3) nearly 50 percent of workers' compensation claims can be accounted for by substance-abuse problems—related medical claims are approximately 400 percent more expensive than those unrelated to substance abuse; and (4) people who abuse are absent from work more often than those who do not by an average of three weeks per year (*Occupational Hazards*, 10/98).

When stress from change runs wild in your workplace, people will often find stress relief through the use of legal and illegal substances. Whether their abuse is temporary or addictive, it is frequently triggered by stress and feeds the dysfunctional reactions described elsewhere in this chapter. Use of even the most accepted substances—coffee, cigarettes, and alcohol—can lead to dysfunctional outcomes at work. Take your role in the implementation of major change, for example. Those late nights fed by hot coffee? Every substance, coffee included, has a *rebound effect*: After your body has metabolized the ingested substance, it falls back to a point of energy and vigor that is lower than it was before your first cup, pill, or sniff (or higher if the substance tends to decrease one's energy). To counteract this rebound effect from caffeine, for example, we drink another cup, adding to the caffeine reaction waiting in the wings. Eventually, after several cups, we might feel "wired," agitated, and even anxious. Organizations have similar reactions to the jolts of authority and activity required to sustain programmatic organizational change.

Locking On to Programmatic Solutions

The maladaptive response to stress of an organization's workforce can be measured and quantified using readily available data. Although such data are literally "under the nose" of anyone choosing to look, most people do not look. Why? The answer lies in the human tendency to generalize information and patterns in order to process the overwhelming volume of information received by the senses. Imagine, for example, what it would be like were you not able to intuitively understand that the cars whizzing past on the freeway would cause you severe physical harm were you to encounter the fender of one in midjourney down your neighborhood's street? Our minds, quite on their own, learn to create mental models out of our experience and apply those models to novel yet related situations, thereby increasing the speed with which the new information can be processed and readied for decision making. Effective managers do this well; were they not able to do so, they would be stymied by every novel situation. Like every strength, however, it contains the seeds of its own greatest weakness. A mental model about the causes of workplace accidents can produce a self-perpetuating spiral of cause and effect actions leading to tragedy.

If you are like most people, you probably believe that some combination of dangerous equipment and faulty operation causes accidents. And you would not be wrong. In the case of this conclusion, generalization is an efficient and accurate cognitive function. Next...what should be done to decrease the number of accidents in the workplace? Once again, your mind cannot help but generalize. Like most, again, you probably adopt a cause-effect generalization while in search of a solution. Because your initial generalization offered dangerous equipment and faulty operation as causes, you will likely think of the following two options for the minimization of accidents in the workplace: (1) audit the equipment to ensure safety and replace dangerous machines and environmental conditions; and (2) train operators on the proper operation of the machinery. Were you to take this approach, you would most certainly reduce the number of accidents to a "manageable" number. You would walk away with satisfaction stemming from the knowledge that you have helped to create a safer workplace.

What would you then do if you discovered an increase in accidents in another area of your company? Quite obviously, you would take actions similar to those that worked so well previously. And, in most cases, you probably would realize a similar reduction in accidents. The cause-effect treatment will have been sufficiently reinforced, and, given your mind's ability to economize with its perceptions and cognitions, you will have developed a tendency to see accidents as deficits in safety and training; you will have developed a mental model for the reduction of workplace accidents. In various areas of your organization, your treatment is bound to work less well than in others. Like most who discover this less-than-expected improvement, you will press for closer examination of the equipment or still better operator training. Should accident rates decline more slowly than expected, or even increase, you may determine that the real cause is the fact that operators do not pay attention during safety trainings. So, you create a test for them to take at the end of each training, thereby holding them accountable for their learning. As accident rate reductions continue to underwhelm, you hold managers accountable for the rates in their areas; you make a few visible transfers of managers who cannot decrease rates in their areas and you offer free meals out for teams with the best safety records. You may even reorganize the area, putting it under the watch of a manager with a superb track record for safety. You expend great time, energy, personnel, and expense to finally see the changes you require.

Outcomes in the next "low-performing" shop were not quite so successful. Your now fully reinforced mental model for the treatment of safety shortcomings blinds you to the fact that the organizational structure put in place six months before the increase in accident rates changed the composition of the teams, forcing experienced workers to team up with new employees. At the same time, the new government contract increased the production level by 10 percent, and workers not used to working together found themselves facing increased quotas and increased pressure for production. Established patterns developed over the years between long-time co-workers were lost as new people and processes were put in place. Out of fear, your managers pushed hard on production targets and relied on the programmatic safety training programs to bring a "culture of safety" back into the area. They missed the fact that the mandatory training removed bodies from the line just when their production targets were at their peak. Safety seemed a lesser priority.

Managers, with the best intentions, offered social rewards for productivity—teams and individuals were acknowledged publicly for their efforts. When others tried to keep up, accidents increased—small ones, at first. Then the auditors came and asked volumes of questions about machines and procedures. Answering their questions took time. Having them onsite added to the newness of the situation for the employees. It took time to attend safety training classes, too, which only increased the pressure. Then, when senior management became involved and removed the underperforming managers, the new management had to get up to speed on both the production processes and on dynamics of the new team. As the minor accidents continued, the pressure for zero tolerance became severe, only adding to the stress. By the time the foreman lost his finger in a press, the situation had reached fever pitch. When OSHA closed the shop, the contract was lost.

What Went Wrong?

Leadership had learned to generalize a solution from one situation to the next. Generalization permitted rapid response to safety problems in all but a few shops. Unfortunately, the treatment, in the last shop, was worse than the disease. What was needed was not enforced accountability to the now centralized safety program. Programmatic change only worsened the situation.

CONCLUSION

Programmatic change is a generalized response to a felt or perceived organizational need or issue. Unfortunately, the difficulties caused by this type of change add unnecessary resistance, delay, and cost to change programs, thereby reducing their effectiveness and credibility and that of those who sponsor the changes. Resistance to organizational change creates stress in the workplace, and stress is a tremendous burden on our organizations. Seventy-eight percent of Americans describe their jobs as stressful, with 40 percent indicating very high to extremely high levels of stress at work, while only 25 percent report being "extremely satisfied" with their jobs. It is estimated that job stress costs American businesses $200–300 billion each year due to absenteeism, reduced productivity, turnover, accidents, medical costs, insurance premiums, and legal fees. This amounts to more than the total net profits of all of the Fortune 500 companies combined! As Hans Selye pointed out nearly fifty years ago, we cannot expect our lives to be stress-free. Few of us, in fact would wish this upon ourselves. Stress is a by-product of challenge and growth. Unnecessary stress, on the other hand, drains our individual and collective productivity. Stress from programmatic organizational change is unnecessary stress. As such, it is a direct threat to the effectiveness of the change programs we implement in our organizations.

Solutions to the difficult problems encountered in the implementation of organizational change surround you; you have been trained not to see. Unfortunately, as a "leadership class," we have become far-sighted, seeing the big picture of grand change while missing the very details of human reaction to change that limit the effectiveness of our designs. The solution to the fear found in organizations undergoing change is to be found in a narrowing of vision. Stop. Look around you. Visit your areas. Be willing to "put on the costume" of people in your workplace. Insist upon being trained in unfamiliar roles as close to the customer interface as possible. Listen. Learn what happens when news of new change programs filters to the areas. Then, imagine a workforce able to move from one way of operating to the next without the resistance, without the dysfunction, and without the losses lurking, unrecognized until now, in the cost structure of your organization.

Finding a Better Way
to Change

In any organizational change, the goal of leaders and change agents should be the development of genuine, intrinsically motivated commitment to the new values, goals, and objectives in all those expected to change. In essence, then, the goal of any implementation process should be to win over the hearts and minds of the organization's members. In this chapter, we examine a method of change from an unexpected source that accomplishes this goal.

C urrent paradigms of organizational change use marketing methods to inform and interest, accountability enforcement to ensure compliance, and, in some cases, significant amounts of employee participation to develop commitment and buy-in. Each approach has limitations: marketing increases the likelihood of resistance, enforcement builds both compliance and resistance, and skepticism limits genuine participation. As long as change processes are perceived as being sold downward from the executive suite, their success will seldom reach their full potential. And yet, these are the models most frequently used during the implementation of organizational change. It is as if we cannot see beyond the confines of our own underlying beliefs about the nature of change. We need a new paradigm.

Ideally, such a new paradigm will come from within a "programmatic change gone wrong," for such a situation will surely provide us with an alternative that has practical power. An alternative approach to organizational change that can demonstrate success within even the most cynically received programmatic change has the potential to turn around, or prevent, the problems of resistance surrounding such a change. In addition, the benchmarked example should come from the context with the following characteristics in common with the general form of organizations:

▼   An organizational culture with strong "command-and-control" characteristics and a tendency to reduce problems to "manageable" goals, strategies, action plans, and implementation tactics that can be monitored and measured from a distance;

▼   Changing conditions in the field of enterprise that force fairly regular adaptive changes;

▼   Leadership characteristics ingrained either through professional training or field experience;

▼   Win/lose demands for performance;

▼   Influential stakeholders;

▼   Targets of change who must be won over to ensure commitment and motivation.

While readers will arrive at differing analogs based upon these criteria, the one that most closely fits for the purposes of this book can be found in the geo-political field of the military. Military action demonstrates perhaps the longest tradition of command-and-control leadership, a tradition pre-dating those of even long-established religious organizations. From time immemorial, military leaders have faced changing conditions in their fields of operation requiring them to ongoingly develop intricate action plans to be carried out through the execution of tactics steered by the scalar chain of command. To be promoted to the leadership ranks, military personnel must receive a combination of professional training and on-the-job experience. The demands for performance in the military are clearly win/lose, where lives hang in the balance. On a larger scale, organizational failure can bring the downfall of the organization itself. As seen during all American military conflicts since the Vietnam War, the opinion of stakeholders (e.g., politicians, the media, and the citizenry) weigh heavily on the decisions made during the planning and execution of action.

By these criteria then, we might search military history for examples of situations where a problem was addressed by a large-scale, programmatic plan which, for any number of reasons, created a level of resistance so severe that the plan was doomed to failure. Many Americans conclude that the Vietnam War, for example, failed because of massive resistance generated at home and abroad to the specter of a large nation attempting to bomb a small nation "back into the stone age." While a discussion of the merits of U.S. involvement is beyond the scope and purpose of this book, Vietnam does certainly represent a case where the implementation of a large-scale programmatic plan generated a level of popular resistance so severe that the effort itself was doomed. Within the context of the time, the government and military could not possibly have implemented their programmatic approach to what they believed would be its logical conclusion—victory.

The Vietnam War offers our example of programmatic failure. Does it also offer an example of an approach to the pursuit of central strategy that generated support instead of resistance? If so, then such an example is worthy of consideration because it may offer elements of practice that can succeed within even the most cynical and resistance-damaged organizations.

A NEEDS-BASED CHANGE STRATEGY

The scale of U.S. involvement in the Vietnam War was small, at first, beginning in late 1961 when President Kennedy authorized sending 3,000 military advisors to South Vietnam to provide training and support to South Vietnamese war efforts. This involvement escalated during the Kennedy administration and reached a peak in 1965 when President Johnson authorized a large-scale military buildup of American forces in the South, at first, followed by offensive actions against cadres form the North, then against the regular military forces of the North. From this point until the withdrawal of U.S. combat forces in 1973, the military command structure of the United States continued to see the struggle in Vietnam as winnable through the application of massive firepower and overwhelming force.

Not all members of the military saw the war in this light, however. General Lewis Walt, Commander of the U.S. Marine forces in Vietnam from May of 1965 to May of 1967, believed in another key to the fighting of the war:

> The struggle was in the rice paddies…in and among the people, not passing through, but living among them, night and day…and joining with them in steps toward a better life long overdue…(Maitland, 1983).

While the U.S. Army pursued a policy designed to destroy the North Vietnamese military infrastructure, a small segment of the Marine Corps that landed en masse in 1965 formed into small squads, which, when paired with local forces in selected South Vietnamese hamlets, were known as Combined Action Platoons (CAPs).

By 1965, when the CAPs were formed, many South Vietnamese villagers lived in nearly constant terror of the forces of the North Vietnamese National Liberation Front (NLF) or in fear of being forcibly relocated by South Vietnamese and American forces into "strategic hamlets" devoid of familiar faces, norms, and infrastructures. In strategic hamlets or not, the average South Vietnamese villager could expect that the NLF would enter their village at night, threaten or assault fellow villagers, demand rice, and leave with forced recruits. Concerned for their lives and fearful of the North Vietnamese cadres and forces, the villagers had little choice but to comply.

The South Vietnamese military, no great local benefactor itself, attempted to establish militias in the villages. Unfortunately, the poor selection, training, and support of these local militias (the Popular Forces or PFs as they were known by the Americans) left them poorly matched with the superior infrastructure and support of the NLF forces. As a result, most villages were open prey to regular harassment and violence.

CAP goals were simple: (1) secure the villages against infiltration and attack by the NLF and forces of the North Vietnamese People's Liberation Army (PLA); and (2) leave local Vietnamese forces better able to assume a greater share of responsibility for their own defense. To accomplish these tasks, the U.S. CAP Marines needed to be trusted and valued by the residents of the villages they were assigned to assist. Bearing in mind the vast cultural, language, and physical differences between the Marines and the local population, the difficulty of their task can be understood.

Officially, to become part of a CAP, a Marine had to meet several strict qualifications:

▼   He must have spent at least two months in a combat unit.
▼   He must have been recommended by his commanding officer.
▼   He must have displayed a positive personal respect for the Vietnamese people, their customs, religions, and mannerisms.

Any traces of xenophobia would typically bounce a CAP soldier out of the program. When the match between CAP marines and their PF counterparts worked well, mutual trust and respect developed between the CAPs and the villages to which they were assigned:

> The marines liked duty in the village. They enjoyed the admiration of the PFs who were unwilling to challenge the Viet Cong alone…The Marines were aware that the village children did not avoid them, and that the children's parents were more than polite. The Marines "had accepted too many invitations to too many meals in too many homes to believe they were not liked by many and tolerated by most" (West, 1972).

> Their conduct had won them admiration and status within the Vietnamese village society in which they were working (Brush, 1994).

While these glowing quotes cannot accurately represent the situation in every CAP, the approach did create far better relations between the South Vietnamese people and the U.S. forces than were seen elsewhere in the region. Local militia members came to respect the CAP Marines as they realized that many were willing to, and did, give their lives to protect the militia members' villages, homes, and loved ones. In many cases, the villagers trusted the Marine CAPs to such a degree that they freely passed on information about the activities of the Northern forces. In fact, while the Tet Offensive came as a surprise to the U.S. military as a whole, CAPs had been passing on reports of the attack for quite some time before its commencement.

The Marines patrolled in the CAP with local forces at night (with a more effective partnership in some villages than in others) and worked to build trust during the daylight by helping villagers staff and support medical clinics, improve sanitation, build houses and community structures, and implement a variety of other civic action projects.

THE IMPACT OF COMBINED ACTION

While the success of the CAPs is beyond question, it must be remembered that this "program" ran counter to the stated U.S. military goal of driving the North Vietnamese to defeat by subjecting their forces to overwhelming military might. General Westmoreland, commander of the Military Assistance Command-Vietnam (MACV), 1964–1968, even went so far as to say, "I simply do not have enough numbers to put a squad of Americans in every village and hamlet; that would have been fragmenting resources and exposing them to defeat in detail" (Westmoreland, 1976). While the facts challenge this assertion, the reality is that the CAP approach was simply outside the U.S. military paradigm for the Vietnam War. Perhaps, had the U.S. military and government adopted the customizable approach of the CAPs, the outcome of the war may have been different. Nonetheless, the results of the CAP system were clear:

▼ The Hamlet Evaluation Security (HES) score achieved by CAP-protected villages was 2.95 out of 5.0. The average for all other (non-CAP-protected) villages in the I Corps region (the region of South Vietnam comprised of the five northern provinces) was only 1.6 out of 5.0.

▼ Security scores of CAP-protected villages progressed upward twice as quickly as those of villages not so protected.

▼ By the end of 1966 (one year into the program), 59 percent of all CAP-protected villages had reached the highest Marine rating of 4.0 on a 5-point scale. Less than 17 percent of non-CAP-protected villages reached this score.

▼ CAP platoons had lower casualty rates than did other units that carried out similar missions, despite the fact that CAP platoons were disproportionately targeted by the North Vietnamese.

▼ More than 60 percent of CAP Marines voluntarily extended their tours of duty when they could have left to return to the United States.

▼ No CAP-protected village was ever permanently taken by North Vietnamese forces.

Although CAPs were by and large successful, their success was destined to be limited; such was the power of the Army's large-scale warfare paradigm. Deep faith in the superiority of U.S. military technology and the belief that massive mobilization would defeat the enemy precluded any full-scale diversion of assets to approaches not consistent with the assumptions of the larger plan.

> ...the way to fight the Vietnam War required decentralization and recognition of the fact that no one size fits all, as in the systems analysis approach to warfare. What made this even more incredible, in the view of the Army, was that [in the CAPs] we were giving autonomous **command** authority to a "mere" enlisted man. I never lost faith in "my" Marines. They never let themselves and their Vietnamese charges down. Their pride of purpose and performance under incredible odds is without peer in the history of the Vietnam War (Corson, 1968).

Within the dominant programmatic paradigm of the U.S. military's involvement in the Vietnam War, the CAPs offer an example of how a flexible approach, focusing on the real time needs of people on the line in even the most difficult circumstance, can accomplish strategy without resistance. The point here is not to debate the merits of the War but to examine a mechanism by which strategy can be implemented in a way that generates support and commitment. In an organizational setting, those who determine strategy must take responsibility for a sound examination of all factors and chart a course that accomplishes desired outcomes in the most efficient and humane manner possible. Ideally, in the delicate balance between the individual and the organization found in today's world of work, the methodology of change should leave room for an exchange of ideas absent from far too many stages of America's involvement in Vietnam.

LEARNING FROM COMBINED ACTION

The Combined Action Platoons of the early stages of the Vietnam War do indeed serve as apt examples for the study of a better way to implement changes in complex, dynamic organizations. The nameless change model borrows the following learnings from the CAP approach:

Operationalize Innovation

Very few organizations today have money at the ready to support "creative" approaches to organizational change. With each dollar earmarked for improvement, we must remember that ten others pull in the opposite direction toward the resolution of tangible problems occurring in real time. An approach to change worthy of support would remove the distinction between dollars for improvement and dollars for production. Such an approach would be targeted directly to real time problems even as it carried out the more global mandates for improvement.

It must be noted that the CAP approach was by no means driven by humanitarian needs. The Marines initially charged with securing the area around the Danang air base, and subsequently within all of I Corps, simply realized that: (1) they did not have the manpower to secure every village and hamlet; and (2) they could accomplish this task more efficiently by liberating the motivation and effort of the Popular Force militias. To do so, they needed to secure the trust of the Popular Force soldiers and the support of the village populations.

> All together, the first Marines in Vietnam created an innovative strategy that was well attuned to the problems. It recognized that the people themselves were both the battlefield and the objective and that the usual tactical objectives—hills, bridges, rivers—meant little and the usual battlefield statistics—enemy killed and wounded—meant even less (Krulak, 1984).

This strategy was innovative in the truest sense of a solution being developed in the face of scarce resources. Clearly innovation was a key competency of the CAP Marines, as were the technical skills required for battle and the social skills needed to develop rapport with individuals from a vastly different culture.

Trust Is the Fuel of Any Change

In organizations, centralized change programs, complete with catchy slogans and flowery descriptions of "new values" and "new behaviors," are often the exact shadows of the values and behaviors actually found in the organization. This ironic reality makes sense given the desire of the change leaders to alter the culture. The current values and behaviors are often so deeply rooted that they will continue to be displayed irrespective of the slogans, admonitions, reinforcements, and consequences produced by "The Change." People base trust not on what is said, but on what is done. By eschewing the trappings of programmatic change in favor of an operationally defined strategy, nameless change supports the development of trust between the line and the staff in your organization.

South Vietnamese villagers had every reason to mistrust these Americans who were so different. They had, after all, been exploited in the recent past by the North Vietnamese, the South Vietnamese government, and by the French before that. They also knew that the Northern forces would be more likely to attack their CAP-protected villages simply because of the presence of the Americans. Of course, trust is difficult when people are separated by appearance, language, custom, and religion. Yet, trust, if it could be gained, would increase the chances that the villagers would learn from the Americans the activities they would need to undertake to protect themselves. And trust, if present, would open the channels of communication through which valuable information could flow. Trust was the crucial first element in the eventual success of the CAP approach, and it was achieved in many villages despite the barriers.

> The people's trust is primary. It will come hard because they are fearful and suspicious. Protection is the most important thing you can bring them. After that comes health. And, after that, many things—land, prosperity, education, and privacy to name a few (Krulak, 1984).

"Self" Is the Agent of Change

The way change is implemented matters and is noticed by people whose perceptions and cognitions are finely tuned during such times. When people perceive that leaders and change agents are driven to help them achieve success as defined by the line, then they are more likely to reach out to participate than they would be when they see leaders cajole, enforce, or sell a change. Think of the change as another culture. Leaders and change agents will be most effective when they display nothing but respect for the areas and people they hope will change. When change agents demonstrate their ability to add value at the operational level, then the people closest to the work will tend to see the change and, by extension, the change agents, as something to be supported—not resisted. Seek to help, and the change will be seen as a help, rather than a hindrance, at the line level in your organization.

The CAP Marines were generally seen by the villagers as assets in the solution of *local problems and needs* rather than as a force compelling villagers toward a certain behavior or goal:

By ministering to the villagers' health, by supporting them in construction projects, and by helping them to dig wells and reestablish local schools and markets, the Marines brought the villagers a level of stability unseen in a decade. Concurrently, the Marines encouraged and assisted the local militia, training them, repairing their weapons, and helping them to construct defensive positions around the village (Krulak, 1984).

This approach "brought the villagers out" to first observe, and later participate with, CAP Marines in the implementation of security and development projects. Many villagers joined in not because they felt compelled or forced but because these were *their* projects, not those of the U.S., South Vietnamese, or North Vietnamese governments.

"Their" Needs Are More Motivating Than "Ours"
Whether they work alone or in groups, all people in your organization have *some* aspect of their work routine that *they* would like to improve for *themselves*—even your poorest performers. Pushing them to improve or pulling issues from them only increases the distance between you, the leader or change agent, and them. *Being in relationship* with them, being there to *listen*, is all you need to do to learn about what motivates them. Local issues are always more motivating than central issues. When you discover this, you can use the goals and tools of nearly any change effort to help—as long as you don't preach.

Far from being the "best and brightest" in the South Vietnamese security structure, local militia members were, according to one Marine general, "the bottom of the barrel." In many cases, they had been bounced from the regular South Vietnamese Army because of age, infirmity, or poor performance. They were also pitifully supplied with World War II surplus weapons with which they were expected to defend their villages against better-equipped and better-trained North Vietnamese forces. It would be a mistake to think these militia members would have achieved I Corps highest security standards without the presence of the Marine CAPs. However, many were good students and easy to motivate once trust had been developed between themselves and the Marine CAP members. Many Popular Force CAP members became surprisingly effective. Why?

> The big thing about the Popular Force soldier is that he is recruited as a volunteer from the hamlet in which he will serve. This is the primary source of his motivation. When he fights the VC [Viet Cong] he is fighting for **HIS** family, **HIS** home, **HIS** plot of ground, and **HIS** neighbors (Wagner, 1968).

Build Independence—Work Yourself Out of a Job
Any organizational change that does not strengthen local leadership builds dependency between the line and the center of your organization. While many organizations will always work most efficiently with a centralized form of leadership, no organization benefits from the ebb and flow of resistance produced by dependent compliance. Nameless change enhances the ability of your line operation's leadership and workforce to do their work as efficiently as possible, and, in the process, it leaves local operations and local leadership much better off than it was before the use of this method of organizational change implementation. And, most importantly to the organization, it does all of this by using the goals, values, and tools of the change, making final implementation little more than a formality.

Popular Force CAP members were clear about the fact that they were defending their own villages and solving the problems of their own people in their own area. The CAP "program" can be contrasted with the U.S. Army's Strategic Hamlet Program which forcibly moved the South Vietnamese from their villages into strategic hamlets defended by U.S. Army forces. This program assumed complete responsibility for the well-being of the citizenry. As

such, it did nothing to help the villagers develop the self-sufficiency they would need to sustain themselves after the war. It did, in fact, serve to disrupt and destroy the infrastructure that held together South Vietnamese society. This loss, eventually multiplied throughout much of South Vietnam, is one of the factors behind the eventual fall of the South Vietnamese state. Even if the large-scale programmatic war pursued by the U.S. military had successfully driven the North Vietnamese out of the South, it is doubtful whether the lack of attention paid to the enhancement of the social institutions of the South would have left it stable without continuing political, economic, and military support from the United States.

> It was never clearly understood by the American administration, and certainly not by the Army, that the whole American effort, civilian and military, had to be directed towards the establishment of a viable and stable South Vietnamese government and state, i.e., the creation of an acceptable alternative political solution to the reunification with North Vietnam under a communist government (Thompson, 1970).

CAP forces used to say that their goal was to "work themselves out of a job." This goal led to tactics that would have left local social and political structures intact, and perhaps enhanced, had the program been allowed to continue and expand. As it was, the Johnson/Westmoreland vision of the war as a conflict to be won by overwhelming force held sway and the CAPs eventually were forgotten by all but those who were touched by the strength of the bonds formed between the CAP Marines, their Popular Force counterparts, and the people served so bravely by both.

Your Program Is a Tool, Not a Solution

As you consider this different approach to change, remember that the efficiencies gained by the programmatic centralization of strategies for change are diminished when local operations do not perceive the real-time value-adding of the program. Promises of a better future are far less motivating than the pressing problems faced on the line each and every moment of every workday. Believe in the merits of your change, but recognize the program as a set of tools rather than a set of accountabilities. Help people in your organization use the tools, *then* implement the change.

The CAP approach to the improvement of security in South Vietnamese villages and hamlets proved that a centrally determined goal can be accomplished through the use of teams of skilled change agents who *accomplish strategy by serving local needs.* Programmatic solutions to large-scale problems simply cannot build the local motivation and momentum needed to ensure success in spite of great odds. In fact, the CAP leadership fought hard to buffer CAP units from the one-size-fits-all methods of warfare asserted throughout Vietnam by the Army leadership.

To implement change in your organization in a way that minimizes resistance, you might consider an approach that builds on the intrinsic "get the job done" motivation found in your local operations. Remember that any attempt to mandate activity across operations runs the risk of creating the perception that local needs are subservient to "the program." The basic message to be sent during change is that change can be made at the intersection of central and local needs, not at the interface between a program and those expected to follow it.

> You should remember that although we referred to the CAP "program," it was neither feasible nor desirable to take a strict programmatic approach in solving all the problems of the program or its individual platoons. These problems were episodic and varied substantially between provinces and areas therein (Corson, 1968).

Believe Deeply But Preach Silently Through Action

Inside an organization, a change agent with a deeply held (and proudly proclaimed) conviction in the merits of the current programmatic change effort can be easily and quickly marginalized by frontline employees adept at displaying compliance while withholding commitment—a dynamic leading to resistance and cost.

The best CAP Marines believed in the virtue of the CAP vision. Without this belief, CAP Marines would not have been able to serve as role models for local militia members. At the time of CAP entry into I Corps villages and hamlets, South Vietnamese villagers feared for their lives and for the lives of their family and community members. A firm belief in the merit of their work was not difficult to come by for these early CAP Marines. Although sentiment would change for many later in the War, CAP Marines to this day carry with them the affection felt for those they assisted in the villages. Such feelings can be discerned in a statement made by the daughter of a CAP Marine.

> As the years have gone by, my father has had one wish, one dream, which he has been building up to. This dream is being realized right now. Yesterday, my mom, grandmother, and I took him to the airport and put him on a plane which will eventually end up in Vietnam as its final destination. He is planning to go back to his old village and visit some of the people who still live there (Corson, 1968).

The passion held by CAP Marines for the virtue of their work is the element that made them different from mere "apparatchiks." They stood out to the South Vietnamese villagers and militia members as representatives of a system that was worth trusting and, ultimately, supporting. Can you hope for any less of an outcome for the dynamics of change in your organization? Can you hope for anything less than this same degree of closeness between those planning the change and those expected to make the change?

> When the guns are quiet, destructive combat power is dormant; the commander limited to only this dimension of warfare is hobbled. Here civic action, the constructive aspect of combat power, gains increased significance (Holmberg, 1966).

Conclusion

Learnings from the CAP model can add value to the improvement efforts taking place in today's change-saturated organizations. In the following chapter, we extend this benchmarked example and show how the use of combined action teams (CATs) in your organization can deliver change to your organization without a name, without a program, and without all that unprofitable and unnecessary resistance.

Nameless Change for Organizational Renewal

In this chapter, we examine the nameless change model, focusing on the various roles involved in the process and their integration with one another, the stages of nameless change, and answers to common questions about the process.

T he activities and processes at the core of the nameless change model can be seen each and every day in any organization. Any time executives gather to identify the drivers of change; any time change agents develop and implement integrated programs; any time supervisors and others at the operational level join together to solve immediate problems at the level of customer contact, elements of this approach are being practiced. What is unique about this approach, however, is the integration of these three levels of process into a single model that propels forward the goals of a specific organizational change. The subtle importance of this integration is not lost on the informed reader. While strategic models of organizational change garner the support and insight of those at the top of the organization, participatory models of change help change to bubble up from the grass roots level. The unique strength of the nameless change model lies in the innovative manner through which the top and bottom are integrated. Proponents of traditional strategic change models claim to integrate the top and the bottom via communication plans, "town hall" meetings, training programs, action plans, and accountabilities. Proponents of participatory change models suggest that task forces, Quality Teams, organizational learning, and listening skills trainings allow ideas to rise through the ranks to senior leaders who then decide the merits of, and determine the amount of support to be given to, these local initiatives. The experience of many a Quality Team member suggests that integration via these means is frequently less than complete. Said one:

> We studied this problem for the better part of a year. We did everything we were supposed to do. We attended all levels of the Quality training as a team. We identified root causes and charted and graphed every detail of this issue. We knew this problem better than anyone in this company—ever. We knew what needed to be done and we benchmarked our competitors and, I must say, some very novel businesses outside of our industry. We made a proposal, including the funding that would be needed and the metrics we would use to track the impact of the change. We even showed the lead team how, after nine months, this effort would have paid for itself and gains thereafter would all be icing on the cake. We made our pitch to the lead team and they seemed really interested and supportive. Then, word came back from the divisional VP— we were not going to be able to implement our solution. She told us there were personnel and political forces that would prevent success. Man, were we ever disappointed—and frustrated. We've really done nothing substantial since, and that was early last year.

Nameless change provides motivation for change not possible under other paradigms of change implmentation. The architecture of nameless change is presented in Figure 7.1, and a discussion of roles, then questions and answers, follows.

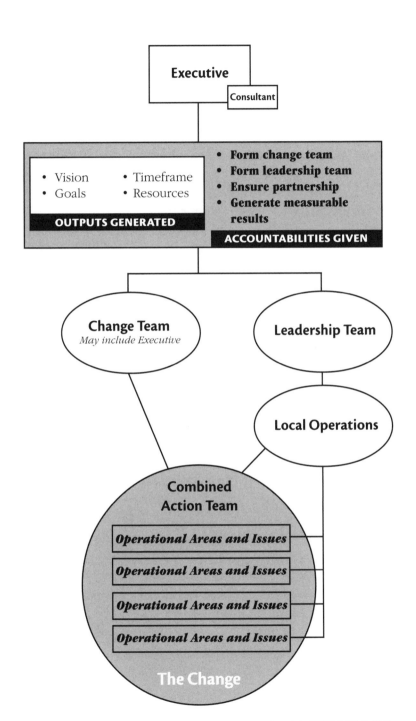

FIGURE 7.1: THE NAMELESS CHANGE ARCHITECTURE

ROLES

A colleague once shared with me his early experience as a new organization development consultant. He said that he initially felt so confident in his abilities that in his first major consulting interventions he acted as if he were a leader of change. Later, as he learned his early lessons, he recognized that he was merely an agent of change. As he advanced to more senior positions, he thought he might finally have the influence to actually sponsor a few of his grand notions of change. He then learned that he had virtually no sponsorship authority. The only thing he said he had gained in terms of his ability to influence change was the positioning that allowed him to advocate for certain ways of making the changes sponsored by senior executives; he never had the positional authority to start or stop—to truly sponsor—change. He said that in some situations, it seemed he learned these lessons too late, believing that his influence would carry the day. In other situations, he recognized that he had learned these lessons more quickly and completely than others.

Before you consider advocating for—or, if you have the position, sponsoring—a nameless approach to change, please review and understand the various roles in the process. By doing so, you will be better able to situate yourself realistically within the implementation of major change than was my colleague.

The following roles are utilized in the nameless change model: (1) the executive sponsor; (2) the external consultant; (3) the lead internal consultant; (4) the change team; (5) the leadership team; and (6) the combined action team (CAT). Each role is examined below.

The Executive Sponsor

The executive sponsor is the individual or corporate entity that initiates the change. In some cases, the sponsor is a single visionary individual; in others, it is an entity such as a board of directors or an executive team. The sponsor might initiate the change based upon his/her/their perspective of what is needed or respond to the initiative of others who have studied and considered an issue. In either case, the executive sponsor is the only person or group with the position to start, or stop, a change.

The Leadership Team

The leadership team is comprised of the executives or leaders who are tasked by the executive sponsor with the planning and/or implementation of the change. In some cases, the executive simply will cite an issue for study and task the leadership team with the analysis and formulation of proposals for action. In other cases, the executive will hold the leadership team accountable to a particular performance standard or standards and will expect the team to assess, develop, and implement the change on their own. In still other cases, the leadership team may take the initiative to study an issue not known by the executive and will advocate to that executive for the right to make a change. In either case, the separation of roles is still clear if the executive has the ability to start or stop the change irrespective of the efforts of the leadership team. While the executive sponsors the change and the use of the nameless change approach, the leadership team is accountable to the executive sponsor for support of the nameless change process. In the later stages of the process, the leadership team holds operations accountable for the performance standards of the change. Done effectively, the nameless change process simplifies the leadership team's work in this regard.

The External Consultant

Assistance from an external consultant is recommended for the implementation of a nameless change process. While on the surface, this statement may seem like yet another pitch for the "Consultant's Full Employment Act," the need for this outside perspective cannot be overstated. While internal consultants are invaluable to the process, they are situated within the organization and, as such, are subject to the pressures of stakeholders calling for a more traditional marketing approach to the implementation of major change. The multiple sources of these pressures can outflank internal change leaders, allowing them to gain access to the executive sponsor. Truth is, one strong "marketing" presentation by a confident manager to the targets of change will produce more "yes" answers from staff than will be heard in the initial months of a nameless change. Such managers have stood as models for the "right" way to "get change done quickly" for other managers ready to use their authority to hold their employees accountable for making the change. In most organizations, too many cultural norms and organizational systems support such an approach to change to expect an internal change leader to remain apart from the collapse of the counter-intuitive nameless approach to change. An external consultant is, by definition, outside of the authority relationships pushing for the familiar, and inefficient, change model. The external consultant does not face the same pressures preventing her or him from coaching the executive sponsor in the steps that can be taken to sustain sponsorship of the nameless approach.

The Lead Internal Consultant

The lead internal consultant works closely with both the external consultant and the executive sponsor at all stages of the nameless change process (with the exception of the initial contracting phase). In the early stages of the process, the lead internal consultant is tasked, by the executive sponsor, with the administration of the architecture of the nameless change approach. The lead internal consultant selects members of the change team and, where necessary, negotiates for their release to the change team. Later, as the process spreads to targeted operations, the lead internal consultant assumes responsibility for the dynamics of the process and the external consultant withdraws to an advisory role behind the scenes.

The Change Team
The change team is comprised of individuals with a degree of professional expertise specifically in the area of organizational transformation and change. Change team members can have *content* expertise (e.g., information systems specialists) or expertise in the *process* of change (e.g., organization development specialists). Often there is a mixture of internal and external change agents on these teams. Change teams are often defined as much by what they do not do as by what they do. Most significantly, these team members *are not accountable for the specific performance of those expected to change at the line level of the organization.* Rather, they are accountable to the executive sponsor for the facilitation of processes that lead to change at the local level. The change team is accountable to neither the leadership team nor the executive sponsor for the success or failure of the change. Rather, they are accountable for the application of specific processes that lead to change. Change team members are not in a position to act as, nor should they allow themselves to be seen as or compelled to become, leaders or sponsors. Lastly, the executive sponsor may fill an important role on the change team as leader, guide, active supporter, or, in some cases, active participant in change team activities.

Combined Action Teams

Like the Combined Action Platoons described in the previous chapter, members of combined action teams (CATs) reside in the operations—in the areas of your organization expected to change. CAT members come from the change team and from the trusted supervisory ranks in the areas expected to change. CAT team goals are fourfold: (1) develop immediate rapport with all people at the front-line of work; (2) help people at the front-line of work find innovative solutions to perceived needs at the line level; (3) use the underlying values and tactics of the large-scale organizational change as *tools* for the solution of local needs; and (4) serve as skilled negotiators between local needs and the underlying interests of the change. For a detailed discussion of the negotiation tactics often required of CAT members, please see the Appendix.

STAGES OF THE NAMELESS CHANGE PROCESS

Eight stages make up the nameless change process. Each is described on the pages that follow.

1	*Clarification and Focus*
2	*Formation of the Change Team*
3	*Preparation of the Leadership Team*
4	*The Offsite Planning Meeting*
5	*Selection & Training of Combined Action Teams*
6	*CAT Insertion in the Operations*
7	*CAT Exit and Programmatic Change Success*
8	*Evaluation and Recycling*

Stage One: *Clarification and Focus*

The first stage of the nameless change process is similar to the first stage of many traditional consulting or change processes. With or without the assistance of internal or external change specialists, the executive sponsor (an individual or group) determines: (1) the need for a change; (2) the vision and mission of the change; (3) the measurable goals and objectives of the change; (4) the timeline for the change; and (5) the specific targets of the change (i.e., those who will be required to change). Because the activities and processes of Stage One are, in a sense, classical, guidance for these efforts need not be given here. Traditionally, however, some form of an internal and external analysis of the organization indicates current capabilities, future needs, and the gaps between the two.

The sponsor, alone or in conjunction with specific others, drafts a strategic outline for the change which is then funneled into specific goals and objectives that can and will be measured. The critical differences between this stage in a traditional change process and this stage in a nameless change process are twofold. First, where the sponsor in a traditional change process may choose to give a name to the change program (e.g., "Focus on Quality," "Winning through Productivity," or "Teams 2010"), a sponsor using the nameless approach typically will not expend effort coming up with an easily identifiable name. If a name is preferred or already chosen, it will remain as a working title only for the purpose of discussing the change as something other than "the project." Second—and this is most critical—the sponsor or sponsor group using the nameless approach does not conclude Stage One work with a list of actionable items and accountable individuals. Your company's change apparatus takes its cues from the sponsor. A sponsor who presents a named program and a list of accountabilities invites a programmatic response from those tasked with implementing the change. A simple example can be found in the company that needs to train its employees on a new information system. A no-brainer, right? The sponsor sets the goal: "Train all who will need to use the system." The manager of training determines the quasi-objective: "All employees will be able to complete practice assignments during computer lab training." An attendance sheet distributed at the start of the dozens of three-day software training programs indicates that 96 percent of all employees have completed the program. Training lab software indicates an 87 percent practice assignment pass rate for all trainees. Not bad. Make-up and remedial programs increase both percentages to nearly 100 percent and the training manager is honored at a Systems Launch Banquet. Six months later, error rates remain at nearly double the industry average and front-line managers take the heat for their failure to motivate their employees to do better.

Perhaps a better sponsor goal might have been: "To ensure the proper fit between the system, our people, and our customers." The problem with this goal is that it does not respect the apparatus for change that had been developed in this particular company throughout its years of market dominance; it is not reducible to accountabilities that can be met by the current system. It is, of course, the only goal worth pursuing.

Stage Two: *Formation of the Change Team*
The change team is chosen through collaboration between the executive sponsor, the lead internal consultant, and the external consultant. Members come from the organization's existing change infrastructure and from staff groups providing expertise relevant to the specific change. The change team leader's role is most critical during the early stages of the team's selection and development. Later, the team ex-

ists as a self-directed entity sharing accountability for the success of the change with the leadership team.

After the team has been selected, it attends an intensive experiential training designed to develop the following competencies:

▼ Basic consulting skills
▼ Problem-solving skills
▼ Negotiation skills
▼ Understanding of the operations culture

This training prepares team members for their role as intermediaries between the underlying goals and interests of the change and the day-to-day needs of line personnel in the operations. This role is critical to the change process and respects the *reality* that the process of organizational change is actually a *negotiation* between the interests of the sponsors and the interests of those being asked to change. Behind the mandates for change, task forces, and planning groups lie countless negotiations regarding implementation of the change. Such negotiations are often obscured by compliance, but they do exist. Leaders and change agents mistake compliance for the negotiated agreements necessary for committed joint action. For those who doubt the reality of this assertion, witness the statement made by one man who, in 1970, chose between working for an organization in the midst of a change or re-activating himself in the military and, in all probability, being shipped off to Vietnam:

> I lasted seven months as a civilian. Selling detergent only leads to the exalted responsibility of supervising other salesmen, and this just wasn't for me. When my company's district office launched its "Make W.A.R. (We Are Relentless), not Love" campaign to boost sales, I called Washington and requested immediate recall to active duty (Herrington, 1982).

Like many employees in the midst of programmatic organizational improvement efforts, this person saw the program as an "either/or" choice—"Either I buy-in or I leave." People experience the same dilemma even during so-called participatory methods of change. Nameless change helps the entire change infrastructure recognize, respect, and manage *paradox*, the non-exclusive existence of seemingly exclusive positions. The nameless change architecture refuses to allow "rationality" to destroy paradoxes which, if examined closely, might actually yield positive benefit to the change process and, by extension, to the entire organization.

During the formation of the change team, team members learn how to use particular negotiation skills to enrich the change through paradox. Concepts underlying this training are presented in the Appendix.

Stage Three: *Preparation of the Leadership Team*
The leadership team is the body that oversees activities of all the operations expected to be affected by the change. For example, if the change will affect an entire organization or division, then the standing group of executives or general managers, respectively, will be identified as the leadership team for the change. If, on the other hand, the change will affect distributed functions, such as IS teams or finance personnel throughout the entire organization, then the leadership team will be comprised of the positions at the top of those functions. In a matrixed structure, the most appropriate leadership team is the first group of leaders or executives that sit atop *both* line and staff functions. Leadership teams in matrixed organizations will generally be higher up in the organizational structure than those in non-matrixed organizations. The general criteria for identification or creation of a leadership team is to utilize the team at the first level above all organizational

elements identified as targets for the change. This is imperative, particularly in the nameless change approach, because the core of the process can involve negotiation between the goals of the change and the realities of frontline activity. If the most relevant leaders are not on board with the process (and they should be actively sponsored in this regard by the senior sponsor), then they can assert their authority on either side of the negotiation thereby politicizing the process and increasing the likelihood of resistance.

To be prepared for their role, the leadership team attends a two-day event with the senior members of the change team, the first day of which is introduced and attended by the senior executive sponsor (if an executive team is sponsor, then the senior executive team member initiates and attends). During the event, the following topics are covered:

▼ Senior executive sponsorship of the change and the change process;

▼ Overview of the mission, goals, objectives, and timeline of the change;

▼ Overview of the nameless change process;

▼ Leadership team roles and accountabilities;

▼ Overview of the mechanisms of nameless change (CATs, values, tools, problem solving, negotiation, and the channeling and integration of needs and interests amongst all levels in the process);

▼ Evaluation tools and processes.

Stage Four: *The Offsite Planning Meeting*
Once identified, the leadership team, the change team, and senior sponsor meet at an offsite planning meeting to specify the goals and interests of the change. After the change planning completed in Stage One, this event is the single most significant event in the pre-implementation

stage. It is also the part of the process and the stage of planning that most clearly differentiates the nameless change approach from any other model of change.

The main purpose of the offsite event is to clarify and add richness to the underlying interests behind the sponsor's vision for the change and to solidify everyone's understanding of the process to be followed for the implementation of the particular change content. While the external consultant brings a design for the event, the change team itself is responsible for facilitating the sponsor and the leadership team in the examination and expression of underlying interests. The change team is trained for this role during its training program. The team's leadership of this process during the offsite event prepares it for this same role during the implementation stage of the nameless change process.

The product of the offsite event is a comprehensive definition of the change, a clear set of statements of the underlying interests behind the definition of the change, a proposed list of CAT members, roles and responsibilities for the change process, and clear methodologies for measuring the outcomes of the change. CATs will use the output of this meeting as the core of their activities in the operations.

Stage Five: *Selection and Training of Combined Action Teams*
Combined action team member candidates for targeted operations are interviewed immediately after the offsite meeting. The number and distribution of the teams varies based upon several factors, including the number and size of operations to be affected and the time frame for the change. A large organization with many operational areas expected to change in a relatively short length of time will require more teams than will another organization with fewer affected areas and a longer time frame.

Combined action teams are comprised of at least one

change team member and from two to four supervisory-level members of the local operations expected to change. The supervisors selected for the CAT must be widely seen as technically competent and respected by people who work for them. They must have good people skills and be no-nonsense contributors who are known for their ability to get the job done on a daily basis. Although operations CAT members are selected during the offsite meeting, they must not be seen by people as being biased toward management. They must be seen as champions of the line. Better still, supervisors with a healthy cynicism about executive processes would make nice models for the operations they serve on the CAT. Like members of the Combined Action Platoons described in the previous chapter, these "Popular Forces" in the local area operations are selected because they are highly motivated to work for the effectiveness and success of those they supervise and because they are trusted. Those seen by others as "in it for the glory" and for the visibility of working with management and executive leadership may not be trusted (see *Attribution Theory*). Because the support and approval of people asked to change leads to implemented change without typical resistance, the selection of credible CAT members is critical.

People in the throes of managing the rigors of daily work at the line level of your organization are particularly skilled at: (1) marginalizing staff members or consultants brought in to change operations they do not understand; and (2) making it appear to the change agents that they eagerly support the change. In fact, people might indeed support changes—when the change agent is around. In the agent's absence, however, the pressures of the minutiae of work can quickly erase the best of intentions. To be successful, nameless change agents must:

▼ Understand operations and know enough of the

tasks, procedures, restrictions, customs, and communication patterns of the line to be able to quickly gain rapport with the people who work there.

▼ Believe in the merits of the change.

▼ Use the underlying interests of the change as tools to solve local problems at the operational level.

The CAT training grounds team members in the culture of operations, the interests of the change, and the negotiation and problem-solving tools they will use to help meet local operational needs via the merits of the change.

Stage Six: *CAT Insertion in the Operations*
In this stage, CATs are distributed to their assigned operational areas. Like the Combined Action Platoons, CATs are housed in the operations at the operational level, rather than in the staff areas of the central or operational administration. It is important to note that the CAT itself is housed, not necessarily the supervisory members of the team who should remain with their areas. While these CAT members will experience their role as being somewhat matrixed between their primary assignment and their role in the CAT, the change team representatives *must be located as close to the line as possible in the operations to be affected by the change.*

The CAT *must* be perceived by people at the local level of work as being there to help them with their day-to-day needs. At the same time, care must be taken to avoid hiding the team's relationship with the administration and its understanding of, and belief in, the change. Nothing is hidden here. CAT members believe in the merits of the change profoundly enough to know that there will be crossover between the interests underlying the change and the interests of line personnel. The CATs' job is to serve local needs via the merits of the change. To accomplish this, team members do not hide their faith in the change, nor do they proclaim the merits of the change in any programmatic way. The change team's first step should be to shadow people at the line in order to uncover the issues considered important at this level (which is also the level where the change will occur). To be successful, change team members must have an abiding passion for the importance of the people they meet and a respect for their knowledge. Initially, change team members are there to *learn*. This is also the most enjoyable part of the job for team members able to place themselves in the role of the learner. Nothing builds rapport faster than one person's willingness to ask for the wisdom of another. During this learning phase, CAT members are building a rapport that also yields *information* about the challenges and wishes held by those "doing the work" in the organization. This information must be noted by team members and brought to their meetings.

The second step of the CATs' work involves the compilation and prioritization of the needs uncovered at the local level.

Step three allows the CAT members to work as problem solvers at the local level. During this step, they identify "high payoff" issues (issues that can be resolved and which, when resolved, will bring satisfaction to the local level). An example of a high payoff issue might be that of members of a support staff who are frustrated by their inability to provide adequate support to a reconfigured team of managers. If the CAT can successfully help the staff solve this problem, then value will be added at the local level in a very visible way. Doing so by using the values and tools of the change builds understanding and genuine respect for the goals of the change.

In most cases, agreement can be found between the interests, tools, and processes of the change and the interests, needs, and workable solutions at the local level, as in the example just mentioned. Let us add that the hypothetical change driving the nameless change process, in this case, is one where the sponsor expects improvements in work processes throughout the organization.

Table 7.1 shows the agreement between the interests behind the local needs and the interests behind the change. The reality of change is that the expert planners at the center of the organization typically get it right. That is, they outline change programs that generally would add value to local operations "if only local employees would just see the benefits!" The breakdown in the change often comes from the resistance of people who are tired of changing, who recognize that a commodified change can easily become a refused change, or who have seen far too many hyped programs lose momentum at the operational level for no good reason. Commodified change leads to cynicism which causes people to believe that even programs of merit will not be implemented fully, if at all. The challenge of change is to maintain motivation at those parts of the organization expected to change. This is made more difficult when the apparatus of change in an organization

The Change: Work Process Improvement	**The Local Need:** Reduce Support Staff Frustration
Underlying interests: ▼ *need to do more with less* ▼ *prepare organizational structure for future information system improvements* ▼ *reduce redundancies within and between functions* ▼ *speed processing time of customer requests*	**Underlying interests:** ▼ *reduce confusion and frustration when serving larger management group as a smaller support team* ▼ *reduce overwhelming workloads* ▼ *increase the satisfaction of angry internal customers*
TABLE 7.1	

believes that its role is to "motivate employees" through education, training, or performance management.

When local issues have been selected for CAT assistance, the CAT helps local operations use the tools and processes of the change to solve their local issue. In the case of the support team, the CAT would use work processes improvement tools to help the support team optimize its performance. By doing so, it helps the support team solve its pressing issue even as it *models* for the team the merits of the change *in practical terms*, not as bland abstractions or "values" presented during training programs.

When the CAT uncovers problems that cannot be redressed with the tools, processes, and underlying values of the change, it acts as a broker to help people resolve the issue in any way possible. This continues to build trust between the CAT and the local operations.

When the CAT uncovers problems that appear to be in opposition to the underlying interests of the change, it acts a negotiator between the change and the local problem. Members work to uncover the interests behind the stated position (the problem) and seek to find that level of agreement between the change and the problem. It is our experience that even the most intractable disagreements can be brought to resolution in this manner.

In particularly difficult disagreements between local and central needs, the change team leader, or selected change team members, might need to meet with local representatives to further discuss the issue and to search for areas of agreement or to request a tabling of the issue for examination at a later point. Again, however, the change team should search for, and act upon, high payoff issues first. People are more patient than we might expect when they understand that our basic approach involves assistance rather than assertion. Working with high payoff issues first helps to build that trust.

Throughout the timeline of the change, the CAT recycles its efforts, helping to resolve local issues via the merits of the change. After measured trust has been established between a CAT and its operational area, staff groups can supplement the work of the CAT with the provision of tools and trainings that will help broader segments of the operation learn, and learn to apply, the core processes of the change.

The CAT is the mechanism of trust between the administration and the organization. Once this trust has been established, the ground is considered fertile for the messages and goals of the change and the traditional mechanisms of programmatic change can take root in the operations without detrimental impact.

Stage Seven: *CAT Exit and Programmatic Change Success*
In the final stage of the nameless change process, the CATs exit their operational areas and the traditional programmatic change processes of communication, training, and performance management are used to extend the goals and processes of the change throughout all targeted areas. At this point, each CAT will have generated support by demonstrating the value of the goals, tools and processes of the change. People whose problems have been solved via the merits of the change can support the change publicly and privately without producing, in the minds of others, the negative perceptions flowing from inaccurate attributions of their motivation. When the CATs are done, the final implementation of the change can be experienced as a gentle passing from one stage to the next.

At the conclusion of this stage, CAT members are rewarded for their efforts and released back to their areas to help others better understand the nameless change approach.

Stage Eight: *Evaluation and Recycling*

Continuous evaluation of the progress of the change takes place at regular intervals before, during, and after the nameless phases. Identified outcome measures are tracked and adjustments are made where needed. During Stage Eight, a final evaluation of the nameless phase must take place including final assessments of the impact of change on the organization. These data are critical for the organization as it continues to change into the future. Without data, future leaders will likely feel compelled to make change as they always have, with no understanding of the enhanced effectiveness possible through the nameless approach. Where necessary, the nameless process may be "recycled" to further disseminate readiness for the change.

QUESTIONS AND ANSWERS DURING EACH STAGE

In this section, we explore common questions you might hear about stages of the nameless change process.

Stage One: *Clarification and Focus*

Q: What do we call the change if we're not supposed to give it a name?

A: The nameless approach does not mean that your change can't have a name. Names are fundamental tools we use to communicate with one another as efficiently as possible. As discussed earlier in this book, there is power in naming. The "nameless" portion of the nameless change process is relevant only to the degree that it reminds us not to treat a change *process* like a commodity that can be given a catchy name to be placed on the tip of everyone's tongue. Doing so increases the likelihood that people *will* take note of the change, and *will* talk about it—potentially in negative terms.

At no point in the process are you expected to hide the name of the change. Neither are you advised to proclaim it. A fruitful course is to keep the name as a working title used before rollout.

Q: The data gathering and planning stages of many changes look a lot like the early stages of good marketing campaigns. Doesn't nameless change have a new way of planning change?

A: The problem with the marketing-like change model does not lie in the planning of change (unless, as mentioned earlier, the hyper-rational search for tangible problems obscures the less-rational sources of inefficiency from the eyes of problem solvers). Rather, resistance to change is increased by change that is *marketed* to people—irrespective of the merits of the change. The problem does not stem from the fact that, for example, traditional strategic planning tools are useful in both marketing and change. Rather, the problem occurs when those who implement change forget to see change as a dynamic human process, seeing it instead as a continuing strategic puzzle to be manipulated and tallied. Marketing works in the world because the feedback is clear—when people want a product, they make an unambiguous purchase decision. The picture is much fuzzier inside organizations where people lack the same freedom to forego the "purchase" of a change that's being sold to them. Strategic planning is a required predecessor to wise organizational change. Wise organizations learn how to be more dynamic when it's time to implement.

Q: Where does the traditional change planning process stop and nameless change start?

A: When using the nameless approach, the sponsor or sponsoring group concludes the Stage One work with a clearly outlined vision, mission, goals, objectives, timeline, and targets for the change. By comparison, in a traditional approach, the sponsor at this point would begin to outline (or charge others with outlining) specific action steps along with assigned (or "volunteered") accountabilities. Action steps are not determined in Stage One of the nameless approach.

Q: Our executive is very action-oriented. She will balk at an approach that seems open-ended, and we've already gotten started with planning. What can I tell her are the specific products of Stage One of this approach?

A: Make sure that both you and she, and all relevant stakeholders, understand the nameless approach, the rationale for using it, the payoffs to be expected, and the potential risks involved. All of this should be understood *before* beginning the process in your organization. You have not prepared your executive for her sponsorship role.

Nameless change is probably very different than any other change methodology she has used before. Because of this, and also because this approach may challenge your organization's pre-existing change implementation architecture, you may wish to secure the assistance of an outside consultant who can navigate the difficult waters of this early stage as freely as possible.

As a reminder, the outcomes of Stage One are: (1) a clear vision, mission, and set of goals and outcomes for the change; (2) the configuration of the change team; and (3) a project management plan for the rest of the change process.

Stage Two: *Formation of the Change Team*

Q: Our corporation already has a well-established organization development function. Why not just have this group be the change team?

A: There is nothing wrong with this approach, in principle—the politics of many organizations may require that the established change infrastructure be heavily (or completely) represented on the change team. At the same time, however, we must remember the three primary attributes of the change team: (1) it is comprised of people who understand the processes of change *as well as* the specific technical details of the change to be implemented; (2) team members are able to be freed up from their pri-

mary responsibilities for the duration of the change; and
(3) change team members must have a healthy respect for
the realities of day-to-day life in the operations. Individuals with either elitist or defeatist attitudes toward the good
work done at the front-line would not do well on the change
team. Individuals with significant content-matter expertise
in the elements of the change (e.g., computer systems,
sales, accounting, etc.) must be free of "ivory tower" expectations regarding the ease with which their methodologies can be implemented at the line level. All change
team members must believe in the virtues of the change,
but not so much that they become preachy while in the
operations.

You should be cautious, however, about an unquestioned readiness to have your organization's organization
development function fill the ranks of the change team *en
masse*, especially if, in doing so, you also bring on board
the assumptions and political relationships vested in traditional approaches to change.

Q: If the change team members are so good at what
they already do when it comes to implementing
change, why do they require such an extensive training
program?

A: The need for training in no way disregards the expertise brought by change team members to their
work. Because few change team members are likely to
have participated in prior nameless change approaches,
the training period ensures the development of specific
competencies needed for their work.

Q: As the Director of Organizational Effectiveness for my corporation, I don't think it's wise to have an external consultant play the role of change team leader. It seems to me that gives too much responsibility to someone external to the organization.

A: The role of the change team is to form, train, and lead the combined action teams. The early stages of the nameless approach are distinct enough from other change models that the change team must be "led" by someone familiar with the process. The external consultant understands, however, that her or his role is to be a guide, a trainer, or a facilitator—not a leader *per se*. The change team leader's role in no way involves the making of any decisions about human, material, or financial resources. The external consultant acts in a manner consistent with the prevailing roles and norms of external organization development consulting.

As soon as the change teams are trained and distributed throughout the targeted operations, the external consultant's work as the "leader" of the change team is concluded and the consultant steps back into a more purely consultative position to the change.

In nameless change, everyone owns responsibility for improved performance. The executive is accountable for the process and for making sure required resources are available. The leadership team is accountable for providing access and support for the change team. The change team is accountable for bridging global and local interests. Leadership teams and people on the front lines of work continue to be responsible for task-related performance. All of this is done in the context of improving day-to-day work. In traditional change, energy is lost because people focus their efforts on providing proof of compliance. In nameless change, energy remains focused on performance.

Stage Three: *Preparation of the Leadership Team*

Q: Could you further clarify the identity of members of the leadership team? Three out of seven operations in our division have to change while the other four won't be affected by the change. It doesn't seem to make sense to expect the division's leadership team to take on the role of the leadership team for the change if all members aren't affected by what's going on. And, I can't imagine that the operational general managers have enough room on their calendars to form another team just for the sake of the change.

A: Divisional leadership teams often face the issues of "How much do we have in common?" and "Which topics are appropriate for divisional leadership meetings and which are best handled directly between the senior divisional executive and individual general managers?" Were the nameless change process similar to a programmatic process that only targeted specific operations or functions, the logic of individualized leadership might hold. By contrast, the fundamental machinery of change in the nameless process involves the application of the values, merits, and tools of the change to specific local issues, problems, and needs. To the degree that value is added at the local level, this value can be shared to the benefit of "non-affected" operations within a particular division—a form of internal benchmarking, if you will. This logic argues for assignment of your divisional leadership team as the leadership team for the change.

Q: What is the relationship between the preparation of the leadership team and the insertion of the CATs into the areas?

A: The two-day leadership planning event helps the leadership team understand the basic outlines of the change process model, including the roles, activities, and accountabilities of combined action teams (CATs) in their areas. Consider the training to be a process overview for the leadership team with the real work of CAT insertion planning being done during logistics discussions between the lead internal consultant (with the role now fully transitioned over to the senior internal change team member), the leadership team member(s) responsible for targeted areas, and the external consultant.

Stage Four: *The Offsite Planning Meeting*

Q: Who leads the two-day offsite planning meeting?

A: The external consultant facilitates planning sessions between the change team leader, the senior executive sponsor, and the leadership team leader. Joint planning leads to shared implementation of the event. Wherever possible, change team members (not the external consultant) lead the event itself. Previous training provided to change team members by the external consultant, combined with pre-event planning with the consultant, prepares the change team for this role.

Q: Our managers seem to see the CAT as similar to the task forces we frequently use to solve major problems and to implement changes. Several already have come to me with supervisors they believe could benefit from

CAT membership as a "developmental experience." From what we learned during our two-day training, I can see how the negotiation and problem-solving approach used by the CAT would give invaluable developmental experience to supervisors who need that extra nudge to help their performance. When I discussed this with the change team leader, he advised me to reject the nomination of these supervisors. I'm still not sure I understand why; after all, the training we received was superb. Why couldn't the change team work its miracles with these supervisors?

A: It sounds like you have a strong interest in providing a rich developmental experience for supervisors who could use some assistance. That is wise. Participation on a CAT certainly would give them invaluable exposure to the very competencies any supervisor needs to succeed and develop. At the same time, the CAT must be made up of supervisors who are seen as strong performers and opinion leaders by people above and below them in the organization. It would be wise first to determine if the supervisors in question are "high-potential" or "at-risk" performers. The former, if well regarded by all, can be fine candidates for the CAT *if they have significant experience in the organization.* New hires or transfers do not make good choices for the CAT, whose members must be well known and well regarded. The latter, the "at-risk" supervisors, will benefit from *participation with*, rather than *participation on*, the CAT. At-risk supervisors can be assigned to work with the CAT but should not be given a role on the team itself. If an at-risk supervisor does not manage an area targeted for change, she or he can still assist the team, but only as a "data gatherer"—extra eyes and ears for the team— never as one performing the negotiating and problem-solving tasks of the CAT member.

Q: I am the senior internal member of the change team who will be taking over as the external consultant transitions out of the role. The leadership team in a division that is going to have to go through a major change does not understand the reason for a two-day offsite planning event to help team members "better understand their roles." One general manager said to me, "I know what my role is during change—it's to make sure that all of my managers attend briefings, their employees receive training on the new system, and our division hits our targets. The rest is just a gigantic waste of time. What's to know?" How do I help him understand that his usual approach is likely to increase resistance to this change?

A: You don't. It's not your job. Initial contracting with the senior executive sponsor makes it clear that the sponsor will hold all leaders accountable for behaviors that are supportive of the nameless change process. This leader knows he will have to attend the two-day session in spite of his reluctance. You are making a fundamental consultant's error—that is, believing you have sponsorship authority. You do not.

Major change programs are usually kicked off by the senior executive sponsor, who typically delegates change management to the human resource staff, who are then expected to support leaders as they implement the change. In reality, many changes are politically charged and leave the human resource and operational leadership playing a game of change-related "hot potato," with each side encouraging the other to take responsibility for the implementation of the change. Even in less charged situations, human resource staffers often make the mistake of believing it is their job to persuade others (leaders, managers, and employees) to participate in the change. In your case, it sounds as though you believe you have some responsibility for helping this leader understand what is to be expected of him during the change process—what behaviors he is to use in order to make your nameless approach a success. This is not your job.

As a change team member, you must remember to see your role as a that of a mediator between the interests of the change and the interests of the operations expected to change. While it is probably best to defer work with this leader until after his attendance at the two-day leadership team session, you might wish to model certain aspects of your role to him even at this stage of the process. You might wish to listen to his rationale for using his approach rather than the approach being sponsored by the executive sponsor. Chances are, at some level, he believes that his way will be more effective. Why? What value does he believe his approach brings to the process of change in his division? Perhaps he knows managers who will resist the change and he wants to hold them accountable early. Do not discount his experience. Rather, key in on the value of his information. Point out the similarity of interests between his wish for managerial accountability and the nameless change's goal of getting results through intrinsic motivation. Work with him to identify the underlying interests of the managers he expects to resist the change. Model an understanding of and respect for his position and his underlying interests. By doing so, you will have given him an experiential head start on the important role played by understanding and negotiation in the nameless change approach.

Your role in the nameless change process is so critical that a reiteration of this major theme is not wasteful: *You are not the sponsor of change nor the one responsible for holding leaders, managers, and employees accountable for changing.* Understanding this aspect of your role frees you to build bridges of understanding between the true sponsors (executives and leaders) and the targets of change. Any misapplication of your role in this regard diminishes the very trust most required between the targets of change and the agents of change. Your relationship of trust with the areas is the single most important mechanism by which resistance, stress, future shock, and productivity drain are prevented.

Stage Five: *Selection and Training of the Combined Action Teams*

Q: Why are there only supervisory members serving as the operation's contribution to the CAT? We have some terrific employees who are wondering why they cannot join.

A: The CAT member must be one who can gain access to working with local staff groups. CAT members must have unfettered access to staff to develop rapport, identify core issues, and use the values and tools of the change to assist in the solution of local needs. While it is not generally possible to have each local supervisor for every targeted area on the CAT, the team itself must be comprised of the "gatekeeper" leaders with access to and rapport with the line. In cases where numbers prevent all locally affected supervisors from being members of the CAT, respect and rapport with the gatekeeping supervisors should help with access.

Sponsorship works best when a leader is able to hold a subordinate accountable without any other individual, leader, or group "buffering" the subordinate from the leader. There should be a solid sponsorship chain from the senior executive sponsor, to the leadership team, to the line with as little buffering of sponsorship as possible. Occasionally, issues addressed by a CAT can be politically sensitive. A

173

person (not a supervisor) on a CAT may be prevented from access and activity by a manager keen on buffering her or his area from CAT efforts (and/or from the content of the change itself). While a buffering manager could still hope to prevent the work of supervisor-members of the CAT, such efforts will be counterbalanced, to a degree, by the supervisor's level of access to sponsorship pathways. Also, since a buffering supervisor could prevent the work of a person on the CAT who is at a lower level in the organization, limiting membership to supervisory personnel removes a potential layer of buffering.

Finally, use your ability to understand underlying interests to address the interests of employees who genuinely wish to be a part of the process at a high level. Isn't this a nice problem to have?

Q: I am pretty clear about what a CAT does when it faces local issues that can easily be resolved through use of the values or tools of the change. I could use a little help understanding what the team does when it confronts a local issue that cannot be resolved by the change or that seems to be a barrier to the change.

A: Issues that cannot be resolved within the interest-based framework of the process are rare. When such an issue is found, it is discussed by the entire change team. Some issues are so germane to the nature of change that, when considered openly and honestly, they add value to the process, helping leaders and executives make more informed decisions regarding this and future changes. At the same time, there will be issues that cannot be resolved within the framework of the change. Still others arise because of the change. After careful examination by the change team, issues that are not resolved are referred back to the leadership team. In some cases the leadership team will choose to sponsor resolution through traditional means (sponsorship/accountability), while in others, the leadership team may choose to let the relevant individuals understand that their issue will be addressed in another forum.

Keep in mind, however, that the use of marketing and control to resolve seemingly unresolvable issues is necessary far less often than we have been led to believe. *The use of marketing and command-and-control measures becomes a self-fulfilling prophecy that demands the use of accountabilities to compel compliance.* CATs should select as their first projects those local issues that can most easily be resolved through the use of the goals and tools of the change. After several successes, the CAT will develop a level of rapport and trust with the line that deepens the line's trust with those who sponsor the CATs. Experience proves that, with trust, requests are honored, while without trust, they are frequently resisted. And, with trust, people are far more likely to accept even somewhat unpalatable eventualities than they are without trust.

A Word About Learning...
When actively learning a new concept or technology, we tend to test its underlying assumptions by searching for the worst-case scenario, seeking to discover whether or not the new paradigm will provide THE answer to our most difficult problems. You can recognize this learning strategy in the "What If?" questions:

▼ *What if you had a **really** bad employee—would this communication skill get them to perform?*

▼ *OK, I have this problem with this one supervisor who doesn't know how to track production metrics. Will the team approach solve this problem by dispersing the tracking responsibilities?*

▼ *Will nameless change allow us to downsize by 25 percent without any resistance?*

Because we tend to search for the magic bullet, we're used to asking these questions and moving on when the answers are less than satisfying.

There is no magic bullet.

Better than most approaches, nameless change creates the *context* within which issues become tractable and where those not so amenable to resolution can be solved by more traditional means without fanning the flames of resistance.

Stage Six: *CAT Insertion in the Operations*

Q: What is the very first thing to consider when inserting a CAT into an area?

A: The announcement—make it without any fanfare. Let all people know about the CAT and its purpose. Do not hide anything. People must understand that while the CAT is part of the change implementation architecture, neither the CAT nor anyone else will be forcing compliance with the change unless a particularly critical issue can be resolved by no other means. Make the announcement with full confidence in the merits of the change, but make sure people understand that the CAT's purpose is to identify issues which, *from the perspective of those expected to change,* stand in greatest need of resolution *regardless of their apparent connection to the change.* Nothing is off the table. Let people know that CAT members will spend ample time with them *on the job,* instead of in meetings and training programs. Everyone must understand that the CAT exists to join with people at work to collaboratively explore ways in which the work can be done better from the perspective of those doing the work.

Think of your role during insertion of the CAT as being

that of someone entering an unfamiliar culture charged with the task of developing rapport and trust with all the culture's members. Don't lie.

The second thing to consider is the first impression team members make in the areas. CAT members must not come across as ivory tower experts sent to solve the problems of the world. Team members have one general purpose: understand the work well enough that people at the local level trust them with their opinions, ideas, and needs. Then and only then can team members use the merits and tools of the change to help people solve the problems they discuss with team members.

Q: One particular CAT is doing a great job. They're holding meetings, conducting surveys, recommending solutions, and, in general, solving the problems they've uncovered in their area of operation. Problem is, when we conducted a follow-up survey attempting to gauge perceptions of the change, there was no positive opinion shift between this survey and the one taken immediately after the change was announced. Local problems are improving, but the CAT doesn't seem to be doing anything helpful in terms of preparing the ground for the change. What can we do?

A: Contrary to your initial comment, the CAT in question is not doing a great job. In fact, in its own well-intentioned way, it is usurping the role of leadership in that area. Its job is to help people in their area of operation *solve their own problems* by helping them to use the goals and tools of the change. CATs that set up dependency between themselves and people in the areas they serve are diminishing the effectiveness of the change. While they may believe they are making things better, they need to understand the meaning of an often-cited quote from the *Tao Te Ching*:

> The Master doesn't talk, he acts.
> When his work is done,
> the people say, "Amazing: we did this ourselves!"

The aim of the CAT should be to bring the processes, tools, and approaches that people in the operations can use to improve issues *on their own*. The CAT is merely a consultant to their processes. The trick of the CAT is to help people recognize the value of the change, not the value of the CAT. The CAT is merely a facilitator of the development of trust between the operations and the executive leadership sponsoring the change.

Stage Seven: *CAT Exit and Programmatic Change Success*

Q: How will we know when it is time to remove a CAT from an operational area?

A: Another way to look at the goals of the CAT process is to (using the marketing metaphor) see it as *experientially pre-selling the merits of the change* before the change is actually implemented in the area. Everything done by the CAT must reflect the goals, values, and tools of the change. When the CAT has done its work well, people in the targeted area *already* understand the change well before it is fully implemented. Not only do they understand it; they also value it. Such a dynamic is far preferable to one where people who do not understand a change are quite certain they will resist anyway.

Once the core values, goals, and tools of the change are understood and valued by a critical mass of people in an area, the CAT can be removed and, essentially, "decommissioned." The following indices can be used to determine the operation's readiness for CAT removal and a subsequent formalization of change:

▼ Stable (or decreasing) rates of absenteeism, accidents, injuries, illnesses, grievances, and tardiness (because people already know that a change is coming, the rates can be expected to elevate in an uncontrolled atmosphere);

▼ Surveys indicating an increase in positive perceptions of the change extending beyond the CAT's areas of operations (indicating that a critical mass is disseminating positive information about the change outside of operational areas);

▼ Decrease in organized challenges to perceptions of the change.

Other methods can be used to determine the degree of positive perception of the potential change as long as the dynamic of authority is controlled for during the data gathering. Asking managers to report on the opinions of employees, for example, is an approach contaminated by the authority relationship.

Where possible, CAT removal should be coordinated between targeted operations. As in traditional change methodologies, it is important to formalize the change to all targeted populations as concurrently as possible. Discussions at the change team level (coordinated with the executive sponsor) will clarify the best time for CAT removal.

Q: Several employees and a supervisor from a CAT have expressed disappointment that the CAT is about to exit the operation. They praise the process for the way it allowed them to examine and affect their own issues in a positive way and in a way they knew was linked to what the administration wanted to have happen globally at our company. The CAT exit is a letdown. What can we do?

A: There will always be a sense of loss associated with any transition of the kind you describe. Often, the best that can be done is to celebrate success, appreciate the partnership, and move on in the presence of the loss. At the same time, there are things that can help.

First, if the initial contracting work was done well, the change itself incorporates aspects of the CAT process, especially the importance of the development throughout the organization of local capacity for self-analysis and improvement. Put another way, a change that uses the CAT process should not be one that then asks individuals to devalue their own capabilities. On the contrary, the CAT strategy is at its core a strategy of *continuous learning*— the merits of which should be extended beyond the CAT process.

Second, once the CAT is gone and the change is applied to the operations, there remains a need for an infrastructure capable of using global tenets as tools for the resolution of local issues. Encourage the managers of targeted areas to form their own "shadow CAT" infrastructure that will continue forward. Remember, the goal of the nameless change process is not simply to implement change more efficiently—with greater speed and less waste; it exists to improve the adroitness of the leadership infrastructure itself. A dexterous leadership is one that understands the fact that the true target of any change is the commitment and motivation of those expected to change. Help leaders support the nameless change process after the change and you will have helped to make a fundamental sea change in the leadership infrastructure of your organization, leaving it better prepared for the future.

Stage Eight: *Evaluation and Recycling*

Q: We have a situation in one of our plants that left us wondering if we took the CAT out too soon, even though as a total organization we were ready. Although all CATs have been disbanded, we're beginning to think we should reinstate the CAT that served the plant. What are the upsides and downsides of such a move?

A: At the point of rollover from the CAT process to the more formalized implementation of the change, sponsorship of change in the operations must be seen as coming from the relevant leadership teams. Putting a CAT back into place could confuse the sponsorship. A CAT operating in such an area could easily become matrixed, with sponsorship coming from both the leadership team and your organization's staff or executive functions. This is not a good position to be in, especially when the types of sponsorship will be experienced very differently by the team and people in that operation during the implementation stage. The advantage of CAT reinstatement, in the case you describe, is that the local issues could be addressed before being addressed by the authority of the leadership team. In the balance, though, it is better not to reform the CAT.

At the point where all CATs are disbanded, a few members from the local CATs could be on call as a "Mobile CAT" that can be used *at the discretion of local leadership teams* to enter an area to help people negotiate their way through a particularly problematic situation. It must be absolutely clear to all involved, however, that this Mobile CAT is under the primary authority of the local leadership team. In addition, all involved must understand that this solution must be *extremely short term* in nature. A Mobile CAT should in no way substitute for the use of appropriate authority during the implementation phase of a change.

The CAT process is not a replacement for authority-based change. It is, rather, a precursor. Intractable disagreements between the line and leadership should not be converted into prolonged negotiations.

The nameless change process encourages interest-based discussion between the sponsors and targets of a change. The merits of this process enrich the change and increase its "implementability." CATs build a baseline of trust from which emerges a generalized positive perception of the change. At the point of implementation, the focus of improvement is not on the change itself, for all that can be done has been done (and more). Implementation is a management function—a matter of establishing a new "order," a new rationality. The work of the CATs simplifies implementation management at the local level. During final implementation, the more typical human resource tools of training and performance management are of greater value than the more esoteric tools of nameless change. Nameless change lays the groundwork for effective implementation. Problems of final implementation are best addressed by helping the leadership team better understand and better utilize standard human resource functions and tools.

Conclusion

Although the basic principles of the nameless change process are essentially intuitive—there is, for example, nothing complicated about looking for the essential value of a change and negotiating between the interests of the change and the interests of people at the front lines of work—within the context of organizations that rely on programmatic change, use of the nameless model must be done with clarity and sensitivity.

Because the nameless model is dynamic and new, it makes sense to seek out others who have experience with the approach. At a minimum, be sure you work with others in your organization who are sensitive to the dynamics of change, aware of the dysfunction swirling around programmatic change, and open to a new model for generating improvement.

Comparing the Models

In this final chapter, we compare the program-matic and nameless approaches to change, offer a few guidelines for when to use and when not to use the nameless approach, and close with an invitation to join us in making more efficient, productive, and humane change in tomorrow's organizations.

Without overusing the military analogy, let us at least consider the fact that programmatic change processes—those carefully-named, system-wide change programs often kicked off by a Big Event—desire rapid dominance over the field of organizational activity. Without such a goal, the tremendous resources needed to implement major change could not be marshaled, for those acting as the "bankers" for the change would fear the waste of a protracted campaign. As the military history of Vietnam demonstrates, however, such an approach does not always hold sway against a determined adversary with time and motivation on its side.

The nameless change approach offers an option to leaders and change agents tired of the resistance encountered during programmatic change and eager to foster change that leads to improvement without the resistance.

STRATEGIC COMPARISON

Table 8.1 compares the goal, strategic alignment, intervention style, and treatment of innovation and risk of the programmatic and nameless approaches to change. Each of these characteristics is discussed below.

Goal

The programmatic method of change implementation is amenable to rational planning and evaluation—that is, it can be claimed, even in the planning stages, that such an approach *will* lead to tangible outcomes within a particular time frame because training, organization development, and communications specialists assert that *all uncertainty has been eliminated* from the process of implementation. In some accounting systems, the benefits calculated to accrue can even be counted at the start of the program; such is the certainty of success. Because all members of the implementation architecture require success to ensure their personal or departmental success, a collective hypnosis sets in and compliance is perceived as commitment.

In nameless change, the typical paradox between the goals of the change and the perception of the line is accepted and treated as the single most important *driver* of genuine change. The paradox is a source of energy for commitment, not a dichotomy to be imagined away. Nameless change provides an architecture to mine this source of energy and channel it into commitment to the goals of the change. While this approach may look nonrational on the surface, it is decidedly more rational than programmatic change because it works with real, not imagined, dynamics.

Programmatic Change	nameless change
Goal: The reduction of uncertainty.	**Goal:** The acceptance of paradox.
Strategic Alignment: Align with executive and staff groups for sponsorship and resources.	**Strategic Alignment:** Mediate between the strategic intent of sponsors and the tactical reality of line operations.
Innovation and Risk: Innovations leading to efficiencies are encouraged in the planning stage. Thereafter, standardization is the norm. Strategic alignment with executive and staff groups requires low level of risk. Events are structured to ensure predictability and control.	**Innovation and Risk:** Innovation aligns the intent of the change with solutions to local operational needs. Standardized solutions are avoided. Special teams must be buffered, and confer buffering, against political consequences of risk associated with innovation.

TABLE 8.1: STRATEGIC COMPARISON OF THE PROGRAMMATIC AND NAMELESS CHANGE MODELS

Strategic Alignment

In programmatic approaches to organizational change, the strategic architecture of the infrastructure of change is aligned with executive and staff groups providing resources for the change. Human resource departments, for example, house a great deal of the change infrastructure and are accountable to executive leadership for the expenditure of change-related resources. While human resource departments are prone to saying, "We are here to *partner* with our *internal customers* to help them change and improve," the fact is that the true "partners" of such departments are the senior leaders who provide them with resources—and, at times take those resources away. The truth is that, given HR accountabilities within the infrastructure of change, line operators are more like "internal products" than "internal customers" or partners.

In nameless change, alignment is with the goals and objectives of the change instead of with either staff or line groups. The product is the change, not those "to be changed." Both the executive and line segments of the organization are seen as equal players in the production of the results of the change.

Innovation and Risk

A primary goal of rational organizations is the minimization of uncertainty in all internal and external activities. This goal expresses itself in the programmatic approach to change where centrally driven activities are designed to spread the change to all targeted operations in a predictable manner. Innovation in the change process is encouraged in the early stages, when strategic needs are examined and change programs designed, but actively discouraged as trainers and managers are held accountable for getting out a single consistent message about the change.

Innovation is the key competency of an organization attempting to balance, rather than eliminate, paradox. Targeted operations are seen, in the nameless approach, as wise contributors rather than potentially difficult "students." Programmatic approaches to change attempt to minimize variation by making sure all come into alignment with the change. The nameless approach recognizes that alignment occurs when people implement elements of the change *without being told.* The combined action teams continuously find innovative ways to help people in line operations understand, through application to real-time issues, the merits of the change.

TACTICAL COMPARISON

Table 8.2 (a, b, & c) compares the primary tactical methodologies, source of personnel, size and configuration of tactical groups, key competencies, and nature of control found in the programmatic and nameless approaches to change. Each of these tactical characteristics is discussed, below.

Primary Tactical Methodology

In the programmatic approach to change, various types of programs and communication tactics are used to disseminate the messages of the change as quickly and efficiently as possible to all targeted areas. To maximize the use of scarce change-related resources, employees are generally given the messages of change during briefings, meetings, or during training programs where values and skills can be more deliberately developed. These messages, values, and skills are typically reinforced by managers who use performance management procedures to ensure compliance.

Programmatic Change	nameless change
Primary Tactical Methodology Pedagogical/authoritarian. Trainers and managers "teach" and hold employees accountable for learning and compliance. Economy-of-scale programs are used to market change and develop compliance quickly and efficiently across the organization.	**Primary Tactical Methodology** Consultative. Combined action teams consult to local operations using goals and tools of the change. Positive, practical experience with the change leverages trust and commitment throughout the organization. CATs also mediate the interests of the change and the interests of those expected to change.
Source of Personnel Drawn from staff groups (typically human resources, information systems, accounting, etc.) and supplemented with external consultants and internal task forces.	**Source of Personnel** Drawn from staff groups (typically human resources, information systems, accounting, etc.) supplemented with external consultants and "star players" drawn from supervisory ranks in the areas targeted for change.

TABLE 8.2 (a): TACTICAL COMPARISON OF THE PROGRAMMATIC AND NAMELESS CHANGE MODELS

Programmatic Change	nameless change
Size and Configuration of Tactical Groups Varies. Can be as small as a single training/organization development team or as large as an entire staff division. **Key Competencies** Technical knowledge of the change, ability to train others, project management expertise. Must have learned, and must portray, the values of the organizational culture. Must have received training in the technical and value process of the change.	**Size and Configuration of Tactical Groups** While the total pool may be large, teams of 4 to 6 can cover area operations of up to 500 people. **Key Competencies** Technical skill in area operation. Must have well-developed interpersonal skills and be seen as well-balanced. Receives negotiation training. Trained in basics of (and given extensive tools for): consulting and problem-solving skills, work process change methodologies, organization design basics. Must believe in the merits of the change.

TABLE 8.2 (b): TACTICAL COMPARISON OF THE PROGRAMMATIC AND NAMELESS CHANGE MODELS

Programmatic Change	nameless change
Control Control is maintained through frequently elaborate project plans developed to secure funding. Control is exercised through staff leadership by change sponsors. Accountabilities are typically *process-oriented* and may include: numbers of employees trained, training evaluations, number of presentations given, and number of new systems "turned on."	**Control** Must have active and continuing sponsorship from the top executive. The leadership team is accountable for supporting the nameless process and for hitting the hard *outcome-oriented* numbers. Examples might include: cycle time, cost, sales, profit, satisfaction, etc.

TABLE 8.2 (C): TACTICAL COMPARISON OF THE PROGRAMMATIC AND NAMELESS CHANGE MODELS

The key processes of nameless change are consultation and negotiation. Combined action teams consult to local operations helping them use the values, goals, and processes of the change to improve line performance. While trainers and consultants working in the programmatic model may also consult to operations, the key difference is that these professionals generally see themselves as responsible for driving the change, while change agents under the nameless model see themselves as driving the success of local operations. The combined action teams, through their association with the change team, also consult to the interests of the senior executive sponsor helping to ensure that the goals of the change take root in the operations.

When there appears to be a large gap between the goals and interests of the change and the needs and issues found at the operational level, team members act as skilled negotiators to bridge the differences. For a brief review of negotiation skills used by the team, see the Appendix.

Source of Personnel

The source of personnel is essentially the same for both approaches to change. The main difference lies in the strategic alignment and tactical configuration of these groups of change agents. In the programmatic approach, the strategic alignment of the change agents is clearly to the sponsor group and they are accountable for the implementation of the sponsor's vision of the change. In the nameless model, change agents come from the same places, are supplemented with selected "star players" from the supervisory ranks of targeted operations, and are accountable for use of the nameless process.

Size and Configuration of Tactical Groups

The size and configuration of tactical groups in the programmatic model is dependent upon the scope of the

change and the configuration of preexisting staff group-ings. In the nameless model, teams of from four to six people can consult to operations with as many as 500 people. These combined action teams are part of the larger change team, which serves all targeted areas in the organization.

Key Competencies

While players in each model must possess competencies respected in their organization, the core set of competen-cies in the programmatic approach includes those needed to manage large projects as efficiently as possible. Also, to avoid creating the impression of hypocrisy, those chosen to teach or hold others accountable must embody the core values of the change. If they do not, then they will not be perceived as credible messengers by those they must in-fluence.

In the nameless approach, key competencies are those needed to maintain the integrity of paradox long enough to produce negotiated settlement between apparently di-vergent opinions. Additionally, members of combined ac-tion teams must be able to withhold their natural tenden-cies to solve problems in favor of a more consultative ap-proach to assisting local operations.

Control

In the programmatic approach to change, control is exer-cised to ensure compliance with the plan developed by the sponsors of the change. Frequent reporting of mea-sured activities of the change agents ensures their contin-ued organizational viability.

In the nameless approach to change, control is more typically expressed at the line level by members of the combined action teams as they search for innovative ways to solve local issues via the merits of the centrally de-signed change. The leadership team is accountable to the executive sponsor for support of the activities of the combined action teams and for accomplishing the measurable improvements produced by the change.

WHEN TO USE THE NAMELESS APPROACH

This final section offers a few guidelines to consider when attempting to decide whether or not the nameless change approach would be appropriate for change in your organization.

Size Matters

Large organizations are the most likely beneficiaries of the nameless change model. Smaller organizations—those with, say, fewer than 75 people—probably do not need to be introduced to the nameless change approach. In large organizations, the need for economies of scale prevent the sponsors of change from engaging in day-to-day direct operational contact with those expected to change. Such contact is more likely in small organizations. Also, because smaller organizations do not require, nor do they typically have the resources for, centrally marketed programmatic change processes, they tend to rely on improvement approaches somewhat similar to nameless change.

The More Complex the Better

The matrixed organization, the most complex of all organizational forms, is fertile ground for the nameless approach precisely because of the political buffering possible in such a structure. Managers in a matrixed structure can often shield people from programmatic change efforts, thereby defeating the beneficial purposes of such programs. The nameless approach is characterized by far less of the fear and politics that activates such buffering.

Organizations with simple, hierarchical structures are obvious candidates for the nameless approach to change.

Doctors, Lawyers, and College Professors
In most cases, organizations of professionals do not generally require the explicit adoption of a nameless approach to change, except in cases where the central administration has enough power to pressure the professionals to change. Professional organizations without strong administrative functions may already make change in the tactical way implied by the nameless approach. Where such organizations do not already make change in this manner, nameless change may be a valuable option.

High-Technology Organizations
The use of the nameless change approach in high-tech organizations is more a function of the size and professionalism of the organization than it is of the technology being used.

Union vs. Non-Union
If there is a correlation between the age and size of an organization and the presence of unions therein, then, yes, nameless change might be a good approach to use in unionized firms. Should you contemplate use of the nameless approach in a unionized environment, you would be wise to review your contract's language regarding employee participation in the traditionally managerial activities of problem solving. If you decide to move forward, doing so with the full knowledge and cooperation of the union's representatives will help protect against their reactivity later on.

Using for Downsizing
The My Lai massacre in Vietnam was not committed by CAP forces. Had it been, many if not all the CAPs in Viet-

nam would have lost credibility with the villages they helped. If the change you are contemplating involves downsizing (without offering truly valued inducements), then think carefully about using the nameless approach. Even so, announce the downsizing, develop a plan for selecting and removing people, and use the CATs to help implement the post-downsizing plan. Do not use the CATs to help local operations select employees to be removed. And, do not under any circumstance use the CAT post-downsizing to handle the grief or anger of the organization—as sponsors, this is your responsibility, and you must address it head-on to permit genuine movement forward later. Use some other process to deal with the organization's reaction to the loss and use the CATs after the reaction has subsided.

Downsizing is probably the worst-case scenario for the decision to use or not to use the nameless approach to change. Perhaps the best guidance of all is to defer the decision about whether to use the nameless approach until after Stage One of the process as described earlier in this book. A nameless change consultant can assist with the traditional change planning processes of Stage One and can go a bit further to help your executive sponsor better understand the underlying interests of the change. If, during consultation, it appears as though the interests are broad enough to accommodate the potentially innovative results of any negotiations conducted by the change team, then you may wish to move forward with a complete nameless process. If not, you can simply use all of your Stage One work to kick off the planning process for a more programmatic approach to the implementation of your organization's change.

CONCLUSION

The processes we propose in this book build a genuine base of support in line organizations for centrally sponsored changes. While the processes we describe are sufficient for the implementation of change in a wide variety of circumstances, they are not requirements. Change can, and should, be implemented in many different ways based upon the content of the change and the ecology of the organization you lead or support. We are not proposing absolutes. Rather, we assert that nameless change will, within a particular bandwidth of goals, save a great deal of time, money, and other resources over programmatic change. Additional benefits of this type of change also include:

▼ Enhancement of your organization's ability to assimilate future changes;

▼ Creation of a "learning organization" via a mechanism tied directly to day-to-day performance requirements;

▼ Development of the core of a succession-planning system that, when supplemented with teaching and tracking mechanisms, will produce leaders with wide scopes of experience;

▼ Improvement of overall HR functioning.

The nameless approach to change is a bridge, of sorts, between the hyper-individualism of many Americans and the hyper-rationality of today's most efficient, and enviable, organizations. Under the bridge floats the detritus of the assumptions we have held about the "natural" human tendency to resist organizational change. The hope of this book is that you, the reader, will no longer continue to accept resistance as a normal part of the changes you make in your organization. Our hope is that you will see resistance for what it is—a reaction to the *way* we make changes, not to the fact that we do make changes in order to grow, develop, and transform our organizations and ourselves. Resistance will cease to become an accepted part of change and will, in fact, serve as the barometer you can use to gauge the pressure created during organizational transformation. We hope you will find that, with nameless change, you can transform your organization without it.

Author's Preface to the Appendix

Resistance, a critical factor in many change programs, stems from the reality that such programs often present demands to be met rather than agreements to be reached. As such, they cannot be expected to produce consistent intrinsic motivation in those who respond with stress or resistance to the process of change. Persuasion, manipulation, coercion, and "training" often fill the void between the needs of leaders and the needs of those expected to change. Most contemporary organizations have well-established procedures for compelling behavior. Those that do not, or those with mechanisms severely reigned in by regulation or union contract, are actually at an advantage—they realize they must innovate the steps needed to motivate behavior change.

The key to the success of any major organizational change effort is the genuine, motivated, committed support of those expected to change. Without support, the change can still be made—but at what price? With support, the change can be made more quickly, efficiently, and profitably than without. Combined Action Teams help demonstrate the value of the change to your organization's line personnel. When such value is not obvious, the use, by the CAT, of interest-based negotiation techniques will build the support needed to propel the change forward.

In the following Appendix, Dr. Neil H. Katz describes essential skills Combined Action Team members use when the fit between the goals, values, processes, and tools of the change and the needs and issues of line personnel is less than apparent. These same skills are also used in the early stages of the nameless change process when change team members work with executives and leaders to uncover the essential underlying goals of the change.

Appendix

Collaborative Negotiation: The Core of Nameless Change

Neil H. Katz, Ph.D.

Much of the resistance and opposition to organizational change can be eliminated or greatly reduced by following the principles and steps of the nameless change approach. There are occasions, however, when highly refined collaborative negotiations between the sponsors and targets of change are required to ensure the success of a particular change effort. Change agents who bring collaborative negotiation skills to the front lines of change will be able to generate the voluntary cooperative team effort forming the core of the nameless change approach.

This appendix outlines the principles of *interest-based negotiation* and describes two specific tools that will contribute to the success of the nameless change process in your organization.

To begin to understand the collaborative interest-based approach to negotiation, and to distinguish it from the more competitive position-based approach, we first consider the classic story of two chefs feverishly concluding preparations for a high profile dinner between their respective Heads of State. One chef, finishing a crepe, requires an orange. The other, preparing a duck sauce, also requires an orange. Unfortunately, there is only one orange left in the kitchen and no others are to be found. Each chef's stated position, or predetermined solution, is: "I need the orange!" As the two argue and struggle over the orange, it falls to the floor. A prep cook picks it up and "solves" the zero-sum (fixed quantity) problem by cutting the orange in half, giving one-half to each of the now-appeased chefs, who return to their preparations. Unfortunately, each chef soon realizes that half an orange will not suffice.

As the first chef grates the peel for her crepe, she complains about the small size of her allotted portion, knowing that her diner will not be satisfied with the paucity of flavor he craves. While the first chef voices her dissatisfaction, the second throws his own orange half into the disposal with a contemptuous flair—for he knows his diner will not taste such a small amount of orange pulp in his coveted duck sauce.

What happened to lead to such frustration in our respective chefs? After all, neither subdued the other with force to create a win-lose situation. Was there not a fair compromise when the prep cook split the orange in two? After all, outside of the possibility of one party dominating the other, neither chef should have expected to get everything, right? Absolutely, as long as the chefs negotiated at the level of *positions*. Positions are predetermined solutions articulated in statements people use to describe their wants. Examples of position statements would include:

- ▼ "I need the orange!"
- ▼ "I need those resources now!"
- ▼ "I want a raise."
- ▼ "You must change the way you do your job."

During programmatic organizational change, the sponsors of change have a stated position. Participatory intentions to the contrary, the position is often understood by employees to be: "You will change the way you do your job, and your support is expected." When sponsors have done their work well, changes are wise and well-targeted to critical strategic realities. Difficulty with organizational change does not necessarily stem from the utility of the changes being made, but rather from the *way* in which particular changes are promoted and implemented. As seen in our example of the two chefs, the stakeholders of change often move through a traditional position-based change process together and experience similar dissatisfactions. Leaders, for their part, cannot fathom the resistance expressed by people to what are generally well-intentioned and appropriate change efforts. Leaders often feel as though they are getting "half an orange's" worth of participation from the rest of the organization. And people, who often believe they have a good sense of what they need at their level to give their organization the performance it craves, frequently feel as though programmatic change efforts are frustrating wastes of time that add little value at the level of customer contact. In this context of positional bargaining, each party gets less of what they really want during change, and compliance becomes the standard for success.

What a loss of potential! Let us return to our chefs to consider an alternate scenario.

In this scene, both chefs begin to argue and struggle with each other, as before, for the entire orange. This time, however, instead of cutting the orange in half, the prep cook takes it and speaks to each of the chefs, saying: "It's clear to me that each of you strongly desires the orange and believes you have a legitimate and urgent need. Help me understand what might happen were you to acquire the orange."

This request moves the chefs from their positions regarding the orange to the *interests* driving their stated positions. An interest is the main reason behind what they say they want. An interest—the motivation behind the stated position—is the answer to the question, "What will having that do for you?"

Chef One answers the prep cook's question by saying: "If I had the orange, I would use the peel to prepare my diner's favorite crepe and he would be very pleased with me."

Chef Two offers his answer: "Well, if I had the orange, I would use the meat of it to flavor the duck sauce my diner craves and he would be very pleased with me."

The prep cook peels the orange, giving the meat of it to Chef Two, who smiles, and the peel to Chef One who gives him a $5 tip.

Each chef moved beyond simple positional bargaining to state an interest for the orange—an essential need or desire which, if satisfied, would cause them each to let go of their original "all or nothing" positions. The magic of interest-based negotiation is that it frequently uncovers what is most important to the stakeholders and allows people to develop and agree to creative solutions that help to overcome previously intractable differences.

INTEREST-BASED NEGOTIATION

As you can see in the above illustration, there are two fundamentally distinct approaches to a negotiation. In the first situation, where the two chefs argued, cajoled and fought to achieve their predetermined solutions, an unsatisfactory compromise resulted from a "fair" settlement imposed by the preemptive prep cook. The second situation, the one facilitated by our now more resourceful prep cook, followed a different path. In this version, the parties talked about their underlying interests—the needs that would be met if each obtained the desired commodity. Once the interests were understood by the chefs, the prep cook was able to offer a creative solution that was, in fact, very different from the outcome reached under positional bargaining. The second scenario's solution met the collective interests of the stakeholders—the two chefs and their diners.

The first approach, much more common during traditional forms of negotiation, is known as *position-based negotiation*. The second approach, one which has recently gained more favor in negotiation literature and practice, is known as *interest-based negotiation*. Distinctions between the two approaches appear in Table 1.

Positional negotiation encounters are often frustrating to both parties and tend to produce less than optimal substantive and relationship outcomes. In such situations, one party tends to leave satisfied as the other leaves frustrated or angry, ready to consider ways to exact revenge. Or, as we saw in our example, both partners might become dissatisfied with a compromise solution. Interest-based negotiation offers the potential of significantly increasing the satisfaction level of all stakeholders in terms of substantive, psychological (relationship), and procedural outcomes.

In today's organizations, change has become a constant. Programmatic change efforts sap organizations of the goodwill and resiliency required to cooperatively implement changes now and into the future. When a change is given a name and a series of action items to be followed, a form of positional bargaining is being used. As such, programmatic organizational change runs the risk of producing dynamics that can slow or sabotage a change, just as our cooks were deterred from their efforts when the orange was split, Solomon-like, in two. As can be seen from the distinctions between the two approaches, interest-based negotiation allows for creative solutions that are much more likely to produce cooperative, productive, and efficient responses during change.

A COMPARISON OF POSITION-BASED AND INTEREST-BASED APPROACHES TO NEGOTIATION

Position-Based	Interest-Based
▼ Views other as adversary.	▼ Views other as negotiating partner.
▼ Approaches negotiation as a struggle one must survive or win.	▼ Approaches negotiation as a problem for all partners to resolve.
▼ Emphasis on claiming value.	▼ Emphasis on creating value.
▼ Goal is victory by achieving your predetermined solution.	▼ Goal is to create a solution to meet interests of all parties.
▼ Process dictated by belief that one must impose or sell one's position.	▼ Process governed by belief that creative, well-intentioned people can articulate options to satisfy mutual interests.
▼ Relies on salesmanship, manipulation, or lying.	▼ Requires honest disclosure of what is important to you and what you would like to achieve.
▼ Might force choice between relationship goals and substantive goals.	▼ Allows parties to focus on relationship and substance.
▼ Yields reluctantly to pressure from the other side.	▼ Willingly revises position when presented with good options and objective criteria.
▼ Results in win-lose, lose-win, lose-lose, or compromise outcomes.	▼ Potentially results in collaborative win-win outcomes.

TABLE 1: COMPARISON OF NEGOTIATION APPROACHES

A Negotiation Primer
for Combined Action Teams

The keys to interest-based negotiations are a combination of appropriate attitude and skill. Interest-based negotiators put on "collaborative problem solving hats," believing in each partner's ability to understand the interests of the other and to consider options that create value and meet mutual needs. We can summarize the essential steps in interest-based negotiation as follows:

- Define the Issue
- Emerge Interests
- Create Options
- Evaluate Options
- Decide on Solution or Combination of Solutions
- Create an Action Plan

Define the Issue
In positional bargaining, each party tends to view the other as an adversary competing over a finite quantity of resources, goods, services, or outcomes. Each party sees the other as "the problem." In interest-based negotiation, parties view the other as a partner and the disagreement as a dilemma or problem to be solved *together*. To build this collegiality, it is often useful to phrase the issue as a "how to" statement with an action verb and desired result incorporating each of the party's interests: i.e., "How to use this orange for both crepes and duck sauce."

Emerge Interests
The temptation will be to offer solutions at this point. Remember that these initial solutions are, in fact, predetermined positions that are likely based on an incomplete understanding of the essential underlying needs of each of

the parties. It will be more helpful to "back-pocket" these potential solutions for right now and concentrate on emerging and understanding interests—the "motivators" which drive these initial ideas. Interests give negotiators a much more comprehensive understanding of the concerns and needs of all relevant stakeholders. When interests are articulated, the benefits that will accrue from negotiated solutions can be identified.

Two essential skills are very helpful in uncovering the interests behind the positions. These skills are *reflective listening* and *chunking* (Katz & Lawyer, 1985).

Reflective listening ensures that one person's needs and interests are heard and understood by another. When a speaker is confident she is understood, she tends to trust the listener with more deeply held interests. A reflective listener pays careful attention to the content and emotion offered by a speaker and searches the speaker's statements for what is most important to the speaker from the speaker's frame of reference or point of view. The listener then uses her own words to state back to the speaker what has been heard and understood. This brief *reflection* ensures clear understanding between both parties and allows them to gain rapport and engage in the high-quality thinking essential for creative resolution of disagreement.

Chunking, a computer programming term used to indicate the movement of ideas between various levels of abstraction, helps parties to a disagreement move from positions to interests. One of the easiest ways to help a person identify her or his underlying interests is to first reflectively listen. Then, after demonstrating understanding, the listener can use "chunking questions" to help the other party uncover underlying interests. The questions can take one of the forms presented in Table 2.

While these questions may be initially awkward to ask, experience shows that they elicit underlying interests with-

---

x = *the person's stated need or position.*

"What will having ___x___ do for you?"

"What difference would it make for you to have ___x___?"

"How would it be helpful or beneficial to get ___x___?"

"How would tomorrow be different from today if you could successfully accomplish ___x___?"

TABLE 2: CHUNKING QUESTIONS

---

out producing the defensiveness of the equivalent question, "Why do you want that?"

The responses to chunking questions usually contain underlying interests. When the person asking the question offers her or his own underlying interests, the two parties are on their way to uncovering a creative solution based upon the now public interests.

It is often helpful to sort through interests by jointly coding them as "similar," "different," or "incompatible" (Merchant, 1996). In the many times we have used this procedure, almost all interests come up as similar or different, as opposed to incompatible (which is what most people believe to be true when they engage in position-based negotiation). Neither category (similar or different) poses insurmountable problems if the parties maintain a positive working relationship, do not see the world as zero-sum, and use creativity and positive intent to generate good options.

Create Options

While creating options, each party strives to address the interests coded as similar or different. This is typically accomplished during a brainstorming session to identify all options that would meet at least some of the interests. The key here is to open nonlinear thinking—to allow imagination to flourish. Keep in mind the principle: "Invention before decision." While all options are viable at this stage, those which clearly contradict key interests of the other party are not likely to survive in this collaborative process.

Evaluate Options

This is a critical step because "all-or-nothing" thinking tends to predominate during disagreement and conflict. It is tempting at this stage for one or more of the parties to advocate for their original, predetermined solution. This move might be perceived as manipulation by the other party. To avoid this, and to preserve all workable options, standards are determined by which the many options are evaluated. Obviously, one important standard is, "Does it meet most or all of the essential interests of the parties?" In our work, other standards that have proved to be helpful are *workable* (If you wanted to do it, could you pull it off?), *acceptable* (Can you sell it to critical constituents that have to approve and implement it), and *affordable* (Do you have, or have a good chance of obtaining, the resources necessary for implementation?) (Merchant, 1996). Parties to the negotiation assess each option's potential of having a significant impact on making a difference in achieving the desirable benefits or interests. At this stage, we often have used a grid upon which consecutively numbered options are placed. Negotiators then review the options and indicate those which meet the identified standards.

Decide on Solution or Combination of Solutions

Most likely, several of the options will be viewed as desirable at this point. These options might now be sequenced as steps in an overall plan, or they can be prioritized as first choice or contingency options.

Create an Action Plan

Here one wants to be as specific and detailed as possible. Who is going to do what, with whom, by when? What milestones must be reached to know if we are making progress? How will we evaluate results? How might we continue to learn from the experience?

THE PAYOFF

When local needs and issues are not obviously addressed by the change, interest-based negotiation facilitated by CATs can make plain the previously hidden areas of agreement between global and local interests. This clarity of underlying agreement produces both movement forward and cooperative goodwill. Cooperative goodwill is the reward of interest-based negotiation—it is also the core element of the nameless change process and a required ingredient for the success of any change.

Dr. Neil Katz is an Associate Professor of Public Affairs at the Maxwell School of Citizenship and Public Affairs at Syracuse University. In his tenure at the University, he has directed or coordinated six different conflict resolution, negotiation, and consulting programs. His 28-year career of teaching, research, and consulting has generated positive change in corporate, not-for-profit, government, education, and community settings. He is a Danforth Teaching Fellow; 1999 recipient of the Syracuse Community Martin Luther King, Jr. Human Rights Award; mediator; process consultant; facilitator; leading educator in his field; and Senior Partner in nameless.org.

211

Bibliography

Akerstedt, T. (1976). Shift work and health: Interdisciplinary aspects. In P.G. Rentos & R.D. Shepard (Eds.), *Shift Work and Health*. Washington, D.C.: U.S. Government Printing Office.

Allen, N. & Meyer, J. (1991). The measurement and antecedents of affective, continuance, and normative commitment. *Journal of Occupational Psychology, 63*, 1-18.

Argyris, C. (1998). Empowerment: The emperor's new clothes. *Harvard Business Review*, (05-01-1998), 98-105.

Bandura, A. (1986). *Social Foundations of Thought and Action: A social cognitive theory*. Englewood Cliffs, NY: Prentice Hall.

Baysinger, B.D. & Mobley, W.H. (1983). Employee turnover: Individual and organizational analysis. In K.M. Rowland & G.R. Ferris (Eds.), *Research in Personnel and Human Resource Management, 1*, 269-319. Greenwich, CT: JAI Press.

Bennis, W. & Mische, M. (1995). *The 21st Century Organization*. San Francisco: Jossey-Bass.

Berry, L.L. (1983). Relationship marketing. In L.L. Berry, G.L. Shostack, & G.D. Upah (Eds.), *Emerging Perspectives on Service Marketing*. Chicago: American Marketing Association, 25-28.

Blaufarb, D.S. (1977). *The Counterinsurgency Era: U.S. doctrine and performance 1950 to present*. New York: The Free Press.

Block, P. (1981). *Flawless Consulting*. San Diego, CA: University Associates.

Block, P. (1993). *Stewardship*. San Francisco, CA: Berrett-Koehler.

Bowlby, J. (1960). Separation anxiety. *International Journal of Psychoanalysis, 41*, 89-93.

Bowlby, J. (1969). *Attachment and Loss*. (Vol. 1.), *Attachment*. New York: Basic Books.

Bowlby, J. (1973). Separation: Anxiety and anger. *Psychology of Attachment and Loss Series, Vol. 3*. New York: Basic Books.

Boyatzis, R.E. (1982). *The Competent Manager: A model for effective performance*. New York: John Wiley & Sons.

Bridges, W. (1980). *Transitions*. Reading, MA: Addison-Wesley.

Brush, P. (1994). Civic action: The Marine Corps experience in Vietnam, Pt. I. *The Sixties Project*. Charlottesville, VA: Viet Nam Generation, Inc. & The Institute of Advanced Technology in the Humanities.

Bureau of National Affairs (1993). *Occupational Safety & Health Reporter*, *22*(46). Washington, DC: Bureau of National Affairs.

Coch, L. & French, J.P. (1948). Overcoming resistance to change. *Human Relations*, *1*, 512-532.

Cohen, S. (1980). After effects of stress on human performance and social behavior: A review of research and theory. *Psychological Bulletin, 88*, 82-108.

Conner, D. (1993). *Managing at the Speed of Change*. New York: Villard Books.

Conway, T.L., Ward, H.W., Vickers, R.R. Jr, & Rahe, R.H. (1981). Occupational stress and variation in cigarette, coffee, and alcohol consumption. *Journal of Health and Social Behavior*, *22*, 155-165.

Corson, W.R., Col. (1968). *The Betrayal*. New York: Norton.

Fayol, H. (1949) (trans. C. Storrs, orig. pub. 1916). *General and Industrial Management*. London: Pitman Publishing, Ltd.

Fishman, C. (1997). Change. *Fast Company*, (04-01-97), 64.

Freud, A. (1936). *The Ego and the Mechanisms of Defense*. London: Hogarth Press.

Gaskell, P. (1833). *The Manufacturing Population of England*. London: Baldwin & Cradock.

Gilmore, G. (1994). Coping with the reality of rightsizing. *Risk Management*, *41*(1), 43-36.

Glass, D.C. & Singer, J.E. (1972). *Urban Stress*. New York: Academic Press.

Goetzel, R.Z., Anderson, D.R., Whitmer, R.W., Ozminkowski, R.J., Dunn, R.L., & Wasserman, J. (1998). The relationship between modifiable health risks and health care expenditures: An analysis of the multi-employer HERO health risk and cost database. *Journal of Occupational and Environmental Medicine, 40*(10), 843-854.

Goldberger, L. & Breznits, S. (Eds.) (1982). *Handbook of Stress: Theoretical and clinical aspects.* New York: The Free Press.

Gronroos, C. (1995) Relationship marketing: The strategy continuum. *Journal of the Academy of Marketing Science, Vol. 23, #4,* 252-254.

Gouillart, F.J. & Kelly, J.N. (1995). *Transforming the Organization.* New York: McGraw-Hill.

Guiltinan, J.P. & Paul, G.W. (1982). *Marketing Management.* New York: McGraw-Hill.

Gulik, L. & Urwick, L. (Eds.) (1937). *Papers on the Science of Administration,* 3-13. New York: Institute of Public Administration.

Hackman, J.R. & Oldham, G.R. (1976). Motivation through the design of work: Test of a theory. *Organizational Behavior and Human Performance, 16,* 250-79.

Harlow, H.F. (1958). The nature of love. *American Psychologist,* Jan. 1962.

Hawkins, D.I., Best, R.J., & Coney, K.A. (1992). *Consumer Behavior.* Homewood, IL: Irwin.

Herrington, S.A. (1982). *Silence Was a Weapon.* Novato, CA: Presidio Press.

Herzberg, F. (1966). *Work and the Nature of Man.* Cleveland: World.

Holmberg, Maj. W. (1966). Civic action. *Marine Corps Gazette, 50*(6), 28.

Holmes, T.H. & Rahe, R.H. (1968). The social readjustment rating scale. *Journal of Psychosomatic Research, 2,* 213-18.

Holt, R.R. (1982). Occupational stress. In L. Goldberger & S. Breznitz (Eds.), *Handbook of Stress: Theoretical and clinical aspects.* New York: The Free Press.

Jick, T.D. (1993). *Managing Change: Cases and concepts*. Boston, MA: Irwin.

Kanter, R.M., Stein, B.A., & Jick, T.D. (1992). *The Challenge of Organizational Change*. New York: The Free Press.

Kaplan, J. & Bernays, A. (1997). *The Language of Names*. New York: Simon & Schuster.

Katz, N. & Lawyer, J. (1985). *Communication and Conflict Resolution Skills*. Dubuque, IA: Kendall-Hunt.

Kobasa, S. (1979). Stressful life events, personality, and health: An inquiry into hardiness. *Journal of Personality and Social Psychology, 37*, 1-11.

Kobasa, S., Maddi, S., & Kahn, S. (1982). Hardiness and health: A prospective study. *Journal of Personality and Social Psychology, 42*, 168-177.

Kotter, J.P. (1996). *Leading Change*. Boston, MA: Harvard Business School Press.

Krulak, V. (1984). *First to Fight: An inside view of the U.S. Marine Corps*. Annapolis, MD: Naval Institute Press.

Kubler-Ross, E. (1969). *On Death and Dying*. New York: Macmillan.

Lazarus, R. & Folkman, S. (1984). *Stress, Appraisal, and Coping*. New York: Springer.

Levering, R. & Moskowitz, M. (1993). *The 100 Best Companies to Work for in America*. New York: Doubleday/Currency.

Levi, L. (1967). *Stress: Sources, management, and prevention*. New York: Liveright.

Maitland, T. (1983). *Contagion of War*. Boston, MA: Boston Publishing Co.

Margolis, B.L., Kroes, W.H., & Quinn, R.P. (1974). Job stress: An unlisted occupational hazard. *Journal of Occupational Medicine, 16*, 659-661.

Marris, P. (1974). *Loss and Change*. New York: Pantheon Books.

Maslow, A.H. (1943a). Preface to motivation theory. *Psychosomatic Medicine, 5*, 85-92.

Maslow, A.H. (1943b). A theory of human motivation. *Psychological Review, 50,* 370-96.

Maslow, A.H. (1970). *Motivation and Personality* (rev. ed.). New York: Harper & Row.

McKinley, W., Sanchez, C.M. & Schick, A.G. (1995). Organizational downsizing: Constraining, cloning, learning. *The Academy of Management Executive, 9,* 32-44.

Merchant, C.S. (1996). *Designing Conflict Management Systems.* San Francisco, CA: Jossey-Bass.

Muchinsky, P.M. & Tuttle, M.L. (1979). Employee turnover: An empirical and methodological assessment. *Journal of Vocational Behavior, 14,* 43-77.

Murdoch, I. (1954). *Under the Net.* London: Penguin Books.

Nietzsche, F.W. (1931). *The Antichrist.* New York: Alfred A. Knopf.

Nunnally, J.C. (1978). *Psychometric theory.* New York: McGraw-Hill.

Organ, D.W. & Bateman, T.S. (1991). *Organizational Behavior.* Boston, MA: Irwin.

Osterman, P. (1987). Turnover, employment security, and the performance of the firm. In M.M. Kleiner, R.N. Block, M. Roomkin, & S.W. Salsburg (Eds.), *Human Resources and the Performance of the Firm.* Washington, DC: BNA Press.

Peak, M.H. (1997). Cutting jobs? Watch your disability expenses grow. *Management Review, 86,* 9.

Robbins, H. & Finley, M. (1996). *Why Change Doesn't Work.* Princeton, NJ: Peterson's.

Rosenthal, R. & Rubin, D. B. (1978). Interpersonal expectancy effects: The first 345 studies. *The Behavioral and Brain Sciences, 3,* 377-415.

Rouse, W.H.D. (Trans.) (1937). *The Odyssey.* New York: Mentor.

Ruch, L.O. & Holmes, T.H. (1971). Scaling of life changes: Comparison of direct and indirect methods. *Journal of Psychosomatic Research, 15,* 224.

Ryan, K. & Oestreich, D. (1998). *Driving Fear Out of the Workplace.* San Francisco: Jossey-Bass.

Seamonds, B. (1983). Extension of research into stress factors and their effect on illness and absenteeism. *Journal of Occupational Medicine, 25*(11), 821-822.

Selye, H. (1956). *The Stress of Life.* New York: McGraw-Hill.

Selye, H. (1974). *Stress Without Distress.* New York: Signet.

Selye, H. (1980) (Ed.). *Selye's Guide to Stress Research.* New York: Van Nostrand Reinhold.

Selye, H. (1982). History and present status of the stress concept. In L. Goldberger & S. Breznitz (Eds.), *Handbook of Stress: Theoretical and clinical aspects.* New York: The Free Press.

Smith, M.J. (1982). *Persuasion and Human Action.* Belmont, CA: Wadsworth.

Staw, B.M. (1986). Organizational psychology and the pursuit of the happy/productive worker. *California Management Review, 28*(4), 40-53.

Tannenbaum, A.S. (1962). Control in organizations: Individual adjustment and organizational performance. *Administrative Science Quarterly, 7*(2), 236-57.

Thompson, J.D. (1967). *Organizations in Action.* New York: McGraw-Hill.

Thompson, R. (1970). *Revolutionary War in World Strategy.* New York: Taplinger.

Tichy, N.M. & Devanna, M.A. (1986). *The Transformational Leader.* New York: John Wiley & Sons.

Ullman, H.K., Wade, J.P. et. al (1996). *Shock and Awe: Achieving rapid dominance.* Washington, DC: Center for Advanced Concepts and Technology.

Ure, A. (1835). *The Philosophy of Manufactures.* London: Chas. Knight.

Wagner, D.H. (1968). A handful of Marines. *Marine Corps Gazette,* (March), 44-46.

Walter, R.J. & Sleeper, B.J. (1997). Employer liability for employee emotional distress claims. *Review of Business, 18*(2), 5-9.

Watts, W. D. & Short, A.P. (1990). Teacher drug use: A response to occupational stress. *Journal of Drug Education, 20*(1), 47-65.

Watson, J.S. (1869). *Xenophon: The anabisis or expedition of Cyrus and the memorabilia of Socrates.* New York: Harper & Row.

West, F.J. Jr. (1972). *The Village.* NY: Harper and Row.

Westmoreland, W.C. (1976). *A Soldier Reports.* Garden City, NY: Doubleday.

Whitener, E. & Walz, P. (1993). Exchange theory determinants of affective and continuance commitment and turnover. *Journal of Vocational Behavior, 42*, 265-282.

Witherill, J.W. & Kolak, J. (1996). Is corporate re-engineering hurting your employees? *Professional Safety,* (May), 28-32.

Wofford, J.C. (1994). An examination of the cognitive processes used to handle employee job problems. *Academy of Management Journal, 37*, 180-192.

Zegans, L.S. (1982). Stress and the development of somatic disorders. In L. Goldberger & S. Breznitz (Eds.), *Handbook of Stress: Theoretical and clinical aspects.* New York: The Free Press.

Author Index

A

Allen, N. 71
Aquinas, St. Thomas 37, 39
Argyris, C. 56

B

Batemen, T.S. 84
Baysinger, B.D. 112
Bennis, W. 58
Bernays, A. 86
Bowlby, J. 71, 72
Breznits, S. 110
Bridges, W. 71
Brush, P. 128

C

Coch, L. 55
Connor, D. 70
Conway, T.L. 115
Corson, W.R. 130, 137, 138

D

Davidow, R. 59
Devanna, M.A. 58

F

Fayol, H. 41, 45, 46, 60
Finley, M. 58
French, J.P. 55
Freud, A. 72

G

Gaskell, P. 32
Gilmore, G. 102
Goetzel, R.Z. 99
Goldberger, L. 110
Gouillart, F.J. 59
Guiltinan, J.P. 53
Gulick, L. 62

H

Hackman, J.R. 78
Harlow, H.F. 71
Hawking, S. 45
Herrington, S.A. 152
Herzberg, F. 78
Hobbes, T. 37, 40, 44, 60
Holmberg, W. 139
Holmes, T.H. 97, 99
Homer 68
Horney, Karen 41, 45

J

James, William 42, 45
Jick, T. 59

K

Kanter, R.M. 59
Katz, N. 208
Kelly, J.N. 59
Kolak, J. 109
Kotter, J.P. 58
Kroes, W.H. 115
Krulak, V. 131, 133, 134
Kubler-Ross, E. 71

L

Lawyer, J.W. 208
Locke, John 40, 44, 60
Luther, Martin 37, 39

M

Maitland, T. 126
Margolis, B.L. 115
Marris, P. 71
Maslow, A. 78
McKinley, W. 102
Merchant, C.S. 209, 210
Meyer, J. 71
Mill, J.S. 85
Mische, M. 58
Mobley, W.H. 112
Muchinsky, P.M. 114
Murdoch, I. 89

N

Nietzsche, F. 68
Nunnally, J.C. 102

O

Oestreich, D. 82
Oldham, G.R. 78
Organ, D.W. 84
Osterman, P. 112

P

Paul, G.W. 53
Peak, M.H. 109
Piaget, J. 74
Plato 38

Q

Quinn, R.P. 115

R

Rahe, R.H. 97, 115

Robbins, H. 58
Ruch, L.O. 99
Ryan, K. 82

S

Sanchez, C.M. 102
Schick, A.G. 102
Seamonds, B. 114
Selye, H. 31, 120
Short, A.P. 115
Sleeper, B.J. 108
Smith, A. 40, 44
Socrates 62
St. Augustine 38
Stein, B. 59

T

Taylor, F.W. 42, 45, 60
Thompson, R. 136
Tichy, N. 58
Toffler, A. 95
Tuttle, M.L. 114

V

Vickers, R.R. 115

W

Wagner, D.H. 135
Walter, R.J. 108
Walz, P. 72
Ward, H.W. 115
Watts, W.D. 115
West, F.J. 128
Whitener, E. 72
Witherell, J.W. 109
Wofford, J.C. 74

Subject Index

A

Absenteeism 20, 91, 92, 113–115, 120; and stress 114; causes of 114; cost of 114; in finance/banking industry 114; national rate of 114; resulting from commodified change 115

Accidents 20, 92, 96, 103, 105

Accommodation 74–77; as innovative strategy 76

Accountabilities 5, 6

Action Plan 5

Advertising 93

Age of Reason, The 39, 44

Announcement of Change: "Big Event" 185

Anthropic Principle 45

Aquinas, St. Thomas 37, 39

Assimilation 74–77; as conservative strategy 75

Attachment 70; to Work 70–74

Attribution 83–84; and supporters of change 84; fundamental error of 84

Attribution Theory: and change 156

Attributions 161

Authority 83; parents as 66; power of 66

B

Benchmarking 168

Benefits 198

Bergson, Henri 31

Bhagavad Gita 30

Blaine, David 28

Brainstorming 209

Brand 57

Bridges, William 71

Budget 5

Buy-In 19, 51, 57, 123. *See also* Change: marketing of

C

Change 3, 6; alignment with local issues 8; and attribution theory 84; and resistance 50; and substance abuse 116; announcement of 176; architecture of 17; as a commodity 21, 53, 57, 93, 165; as a process 8; as a product 18; as a thing 8, 53; as domain 16; assumptions about 15–21; at intersection of central and local needs 137; content of 64; continuous 7; implementation architecture 164; implementation of 198; inefficient 101; infrastructure of 6; marketing methods of 123; marketing of 17–20, 21, 165. *See also* Marketing Paradigm; messages of 189; name 205; name given to 53; naming of 64; participatory models of 49; process of 64; rate of 94; rational approach to 60; renaming of 90; selling of 10; sponsors of 202; traditional approach to 5

Change Agent 114

Change Agents 1, 201; assumptions about change 11
Change Announcement: "Big Event"
14, 52, 82, 91, 103; and resistance 92
Change Process: as a negotiation 152; politics during 171
Change Program: naming of 4, 8, 10, 17, 50, 150, 165
Change Programs: effectiveness of 120; nameless: and resistance 86
Change, Response to 72–74; denial 73; projection 73; reaction formation 73; regression 72; repression 72
Change Team 8; accountabilities of 147; and external consultant 167; and organization development function 166; competencies of 152; creation of 151; external consultant 171; leader role 167, 171; member competencies 165; negotiation skills 153; role in nameless change process 147; source of personnel for 151; training of 166
Change Team Member: role as mediator 172
Change, The Pace of 93–96
Choice 20; and resistance: and stress 20
Christian Thought 38
Chunking 208, 209
Church, The 33, 36, 38, 43, 44
Civic Action 128, 139
Click/Whir Response, The 60

Coch, Lester 55
Coercion 200
Collaborative Negotiations 201
Combined Action Platoon (CAP) 129, 131, 133, 138; and trust 128; goals 127; impact of 129–130; marines: command authority of 130
Combined Action Platoons (CAPs) 126, 156, 196; and large-scale military paradigm 130; as innovative strategy 132
Combined Action Platoons (CAPs), Learnings from 131; believe deeply 138; build independence 135; operationalize innovation 131; program as a tool, not a solution 136; self is the agent of change 133; "their" needs are more motivating than "ours" 134; trust is the fuel of any change 132
Combined Action Team (CAT) 8; and rapport 175; and "shadow CAT" 180; and trust 160, 161, 175; as broker 160; initial projects 175; membership 170; membership as developmental experience 170; removal and feeling of loss 180; results of 178; surveys 179
Combined Action Team (CAT) Insertion: and first impression 177
Combined Action Team (CAT) Members: as negotiators 160, 193; competencies of 173; role 177; role as learners 158; role of

176; supervisors as 173

Combined Action Team (CAT) Process: and authority-based change 182; as continuous learning 180

Combined Action Team (CAT) Removal: indices of readiness for 179

Combined Action Teams (CATs) 11, 139, 169, 189, 193, 200, 207; and local issues 174; and surveys 177; as mechanism of trust 182; candidates for 155; composition of 155; job of 157; location of 157; number of 155; reinstatement of 181; role in nameless change 148; size of 194; size of operations served 194; supervisors as members of 156; training of 157; using for downsizing 197; work in operational areas 157

Command-and-Control 18, 56, 124, 175

Commitment 5, 6, 10, 56, 57, 138; external 56; internal 56; to organizations 71

Commodification of Change 51–53; and absenteeism 115; leading to refused change 159

Commodity 53

Communication 5, 161

Communication Consultant 91

Communication, Face-to-Face 91

Communication Specialists 6, 54, 186

Communication Strategy 104

Compliance 6, 19, 20, 22, 56, 57, 138, 152, 189

Connor, Daryl 70

Consultant 5, 8

Consultants 53, 193

Consultation 193

Continuous Change 50

Court: and workers' compensation 107

Culture 13; organizational 3

Customer Contact, Level of 18

Cynicism 21, 92

D

Danang Air Base 131

Defense Mechanisms 72–74, 83

Deming, W. Edwards 63

Dilbert 45, 46; quotes contest 34

Disequilibrium, Cognitive 75

Division of Labor 40, 42

Downsizing 101, 196, 197; and nameless approach to change 197

Dysfunction 92

E

Efficiency 37, 43

Empiricism 40

Employee: purchase of change 19

Employee Participation 78, 123

Employees 5; as consumers of change 19, 93; as supporters of change 161

Empowered Group, Age of the 37

Empowerment 46

Encounter Groups 3

End, William T. 15

Enlightenment, The 37, 39

EPCOT 56

Equilibrium, Cognitive 74
Escapist Drinking: and stress
   115
Executive 5, 8, 10
Executive Sponsor
   142, 150, 164, 193, 197; as
   role in nameless change
   145; contracting with 171
Executive Sponsorship 154
Expectations 33, 45, 46, 70
External Consultant: role in
   nameless change 146

F

Fatalistic Group, Age of the 36
Fayol, Henri 41, 45, 46, 60
Fear in the Workplace 82
Feudalism 37, 38, 39
Ford, Henry 17, 18
French, John 55
Future Search 3
Future Shock 95–96, 100

G

*General Principles of Manage-
   ment* 41, 45
Goals 5, 6, 8, 60, 150, 154
God 37, 39
Grievances 92
Gulick, Luther 62

H

Hamlet Evaluation Security
   Score 129; of CAP-protected
   villages 129
Harwood Manufacturing Com-
   pany 55
Hawking, Stephen 27, 45
Hobbes, Thomas 37, 40, 44, 60

Homer 68
Horney, Karen 41, 45, 46
"How To" Statement 207
Human Resource Departments:
   and "partnering" 188
Human Resource Functions
   6. *See also* Communication
   Specialists. *See also* Organiza-
   tion Development; communi-
   cation 6; training 6
Human Resource Policy 5, 6
Hype 6

I

I Corps Region (of South
   Vietnam) 129, 131, 138
I Love Lucy 93
Identity 85
Illness 20, 91, 92, 103; as
   symptom of future shock 96
Implementation Architecture 5
Indian River Region of Florida
   29
Individual: and the organization
   44
Individual, Age of the 43
Individual Rights 37
Individualism 30, 39, 40
Individuals: and organizations
   46
Injuries 103
Innovation 189; as key compe-
   tency 189
Interest: definition of 204
Interest-Based Negotiation
   201, 204, 205, 207, 211;
   compared with position-
   based negotiation 206
Interests 160, 203, 207

J

James, William 42, 43, 45
Joan of Arc 37
Johnson, President Lyndon
  Baines 136

K

Kennedy, President John
  Fitzgerald 126
King John 39
Kubler-Ross, Dr. Elizabeth 71

L

Labor 39, 57
Labor Market 19
Lands' End 14–15
Lead Internal Consultant: role in
  nameless change process 146
Leader 114; response to
  resistance 76
Leaders 1, 4, 6, 13, 15,
  17, 53, 57, 62, 67, 200, 203;
  as salespersons of change
  10, 17, 18, 19; assumptions
  about change 11; of change
  61
Leadership 5, 13, 124; dexterous 180; visionary 13
Leadership Planning Event 169
Leadership Team 5, 8, 153; accountabilities 194; and
  sponsorship 5; identity of
  153, 168; in matrixed organization 153; preparation of
  169; role in nameless change
  145; two-day event 154
Learning 175
Learning Organization 46
Lewin, Kurt 55
Liberty 29, 39; as barrier to
  change 85

Local Leadership: strengthening
  of 135
Local Operations 8; as source
  of motivation 137
Locke, John 43, 44, 60
Luther, Martin 36, 37, 39

M

Magna Carta 36, 39
Managers 1; as salespersons of
  change 17
Manipulation 200
Marketing 61, 93, 163; and
  compliance 123; and resis-
  tance 123; basic principles of
  60
Marketing Approach 146
Marketing Changes 58
Marketing Formula 54
Marketing Management 53
Marketing Metaphor 178
Marketing Paradigm
  17, 56, 65, 123, 163, 175
Massacre, My Lai 196
Measurables 5
Mental Distress 105; and
  change 108; workers' com-
  pensation claims 108
Mental Model 117. *See also*
  Schema. *See also* Scripts; for
  causes of accidents 117
Middle Ages, The 38
Military 124; and leadership
  124
Military Assistance Command-
  Vietnam (MACV) 129
Mill, John Stuart 43, 85
Mission 60, 150, 154
Mobile CAT 181
Moses 28

Motivation 10, 77–81, 161; by skill variety 79; by task identity 79; by task significance 79; intrinsic 200; local issues as source of 134, 137

N

Name 5, 86; as a source of identity 67; changing 86
Name of Change: as working title only 150
Named Change 104
Nameless Change
1, 141, 142; and change implementation 182; and HR functioning 198; and individuals 198; and interest-based discussion 182; and politics 195; and subsequent change 198; and succession planning 198; and the learning organization 198; architecture 153; as interest-based framework 174; benefits of 198; evaluation and recycling 181; goal of 186; key processes of 193; machinery of 168; mechanisms of 154; process 201; questions and answers 163–182; reaction to 10
Nameless Change Approach 7, 8, 154, 211
Nameless Change, Questions and Answers 163–182; clarification and focus 163; formation of the change team 165; preparation of the leadership team 168; offsite planning meeting 169; selection/

training of combined action teams 173; CAT insertion in the operations 176; CAT exit 178; evaluation and recycling 181;
Nameless Change, Roles in: executive sponsor 144–148; leadership team 145; external consultant 146; lead internal consultant 146; change team 147; combined action teams 148
Nameless Change, Stages of 149; clarification and focus 150; formation of the change team 151; preparation of the leadership team 153; offsite planning meeting: purpose of 154; selection and training of combined action teams 155; exit and programmatic change success 161, 178; evaluation and recycling 162
Nameless Change, Strategic Considerations: goal 186; innovation and risk 186, 188; strategic alignment 186–189, 188
Nameless Change, Tactical Considerations 189–195; control 193, 194; key competencies 190, 194; primary tactical methodology 189, 191; size and configuration of tactical groups 190, 193; source of personnel 191, 193
Nameless Change, Understanding 8; description of 8; need for 10; newness of model 10; reaction to 10; reason for being "nameless" 8

Nameless Change, When to Use 195–197; hierarchical structures 196; level of technology 196; matrixed organizations 195; organizational complexity 195; professional organizations 196; size of organization 195; unionization 196
Names 165
Names, Giving of 68
Naming: as expression of authority 66; the power of 67–69
Naming Change 64, 165
Negotiation 152, 193, 201; as core of nameless change 154; interest-based 201, 204, 205, 206; position-based approach 201; positional 205
Negotiation Primer, a 207–211; define the issue 207; emerge interests 207; create options 209; evaluate options 210; decide on solution 210; create an action plan 211
Negotiators 208; interest-based 207
Nietzsche, Frederich 68
North Vietnamese National Liberation Front (NLF) 126, 127
North Vietnamese People's Liberation Army (PLA) 127

O

Objectives 5, 60, 150, 154
Odysseus 68–70
Odyssey, by Homer 68–70
Offsite Planning Meeting: change team and 169; external consultant's role in 169; facilitation of 169; planning for 169; sponsor and 169
On Liberty 85
Oppression 37
Organization: historical antecedants of 43
Organization Development 3, 5, 6, 49, 55, 57, 83, 165, 167, 186
Organization Development Specialists 147
Organizational Change, Costs of 101–116
Organizational Design 3
Organizational Monoculture 29, 31, 46
Organizations 41; patterns of threat within 82; primary goal of 188
Orlando, FL 29; unemployment rate 112
Overwhelming Force 136
Overwhelming Force, Doctrine of 126

P

Paradox 153
Parcipatory Decision Making 17
Participation 6, 54, 55, 83; and resistance reduction 55
Participatory Decision Making 46
Participatory Methods of Change 153
Participatory Paradigm of Change 49, 142
Partnership 8
Perceiver, Characteristics of 82–83

Perception 81–83; and resistance 83; of change programs 82
Performance Management 5, 6, 17, 159, 161, 182, 189
Persuasion 54, 200
Pessimism 43
Plato 36, 38, 60
Platonic Thought 44
Position-Based Negotiation 205; compared with interest-based negotiation 206
Positional Bargaining 205, 207
Positions 160; definition of 202
Principles of Psychology 42
Problem Solving 60, 62
Problem Solving Approach 61
Programmatic Approach 14, 57, 197; and compliance 194; control 194; to warfare 125
Programmatic Change 19, 52, 67, 70, 104, 114, 116, 120, 132, 138, 202, 205; and minimization of variation 189; and resiliency 205; and stress 93; and workers' compensation costs 110; as source of inefficiency 136; control 193; cost of stress from 120; goal of 186; implementation 15; improvement efforts 153; innovation and risk 186, 188; key competencies 190, 194; primary tactical methodology 189, 191; processes 185, 195; size and configuration of tactical groups 190, 193; source of personnel 191, 193; strategic alignment 186, 188
Programmatic Model: consultants 193; trainers 193
Programmatic Paradigm of Warfare 130
Programmatic Response 150
Programmatic Solutions 116–120
Project Management 5

Q

Quality 3, 8, 46, 85, 102, 142; teams 54

R

Rationality 41
Rebound Effect 116
Reengineering 3, 8, 54, 102
Reflective Listening 208
Renaissance, The 37, 39
Renaming 85; and resistance 85
Resilience 95
Resistance 7, 44, 50, 83, 91, 120, 139, 200, 201; and cognitive response 76; and the "Big Event" 92; beginning of 91; to change: cognitive sources of 74–86; sources of 65–66
Resources 5, 6, 8
Results, Measurable 8
Revolution 40
Roles in Nameless Change: executive sponsor 144–148; leadership team 145; external consultant 146; lead internal consultant 146; change team 147; combined action teams 148
Root Causes 60

S

SABRE Reservations System 77
Safety 105
Salesmanship 57
Schema, Cognitive 74. *See also*
  Mental Model. *See also* Scripts.
Scholasticism 37, 39
Scientific Management 42, 45
Scripts, Cognitive 74. *See also*
  Mental Model. *See also*
  Schema.
Self, Idealized 41
Self, Real 41, 45, 46
Self-Actualization 78
Self-Directed Work Teams
  80, 90
Selye, Hans 31, 120
Separation, Reaction to 71
Smith, Adam 40, 44
Snowball Model, The 23
Social Contract 40, 43
Socrates 62
South Vietnamese Military 127
South Vietnamese Popular
  Forces (PF) 127, 131
South Vietnamese Villagers 132
Sponsorship 173, 175; and
  buffering 173
St. Augustine 38
Storyboarding 53
Strategic Hamlet Program 135
Strategic Hamlets 127
Stress 7, 31, 33, 41, 45; and
  absenteeism 114; and
  balance with work 47; and
  efficiency of change 93; and
  illness 97–100; and substance
  abuse 115; and workers'
  compensation costs
  111; baseline level of 46–

47, 49, 94; and escapist
  drinking 115; from programmatic organizational change
  120
Stress Study, The 97–100
Substance Abuse 92, 115–
  116; and absenteeism
  116; and accidents 115; and
  injuries 115; and stress
  115; and workers' compensation 115
Supervisors: as combined action
  team members 156

T

Taco Bell 16
Tao Te Ching 178
Targets of Change 124, 150
Taylor, Frederick Winslow
  42, 45, 60, 63
Teams 8, 46
Tet Offensive 128
*The Principles of Scientific
  Management* 42
The Wealth of Nations 40
Threat, Pattern of 82
Timeframe 5, 6, 8
Timeline 150, 154
Toffler, Alvin 95
Trainers 193
Training 3, 5, 6, 114, 159,
  161, 182, 186, 200; as
  response to resistance 76
Trust 161
Turnover 20, 111–113

U

Underlying Interests 209
Unemployment: in Orlando 112
Union 196, 200

United States Combined Action Platoon Marines 127; respect for 128
United States Government 55
United States Marine Corps 126
USA Today 28
USAirways 77

V

Victorian Era, The 62
Vietnam 196
Vietnam War 125, 126, 130; re-sistance to 125
Vision 5, 6, 8, 60, 150

W

Wall Street Journal, The 15
Walt, Gen. Lewis 126
Webster's New Collegiate Dictio-nary 38
Western World 38
Westmoreland, Gen. William C. 129, 136
Work Process Change 85
Workers' Compensation 105–111; and change 108; and fraud 107; and mental distress 108; cost of 106; origin of 105
Workers' compensation: cover-age by 105
Workers' Compensation Boards 107
Workers' Compensation Costs: from programmatic organiza-tional change 110
Working: as a threat to life 32
World War II 55, 63

X

Xenophobia 128